Praise for Gentle Eating

"I had no idea that this ***would*** *work so incredibly fast or be so remarkably simple. In a year I lost 65 pounds, and I have kept it off. I look and feel like a different person."*

Dwight Bain
Director, Orlando
Counseling Center

"The Gentle Eating *plan is where all your dieting schemes come to an end.* Gentle Eating *teaches you that it's not what you eat but what's eating you that really matters. After going on the plan I lost 35 pounds. The cookbook section is more than thorough, and wait till you taste some of the low-fat and fat-free recipes. The fact is, the* Gentle Eating *plan really works!"*

Jim Cress
Host, Minirth Meier
New Life Clinic radio
program

"Since cutting the fat and exercising regularly on the Gentle Eating *plan, I have lost 24 pounds."*

Pina Witherington

"I lost 16 pounds in 26 weeks. Because of the Gentle Eating *program, I have kept those extra pounds off. I've enjoyed changing the way I choose what I eat. Now it is a way of life for me."*

Sonja Peterson

"After committing to the Gentle Eating *plan, for the first time in my life, I'm not feeding my feelings. I'm beginning a new way of life."*

Donna Shelley

"*The* Gentle Eating *program is perfect to use with a weight-loss support group. As the facilitator of such a group, I have seen people who have struggled with their weight for years gradually and gently achieve their weight-loss goal.*"

Judy Peterson

"*The* Gentle Eating *plan changes the way you feel about yourself and shows you how to make significant choices that will build your confidence and help you experience freedom from the inside out.*"

Total Wellness

"*The most striking feature about* Gentle Eating *is the gentle, relaxed, encouraging attitude the authors take toward the reader seeking weight loss. Perhaps this is because the authors themselves have experienced significant weight loss.*"

The Texas Messenger

Gentle EATING

STEPHEN ARTERBURN
MARY EHEMANN
VIVIAN LAMPHEAR, Ph.D.

OLIVER
NELSON

THOMAS NELSON PUBLISHERS
Nashville • Atlanta • London • Vancouver

Copyright © 1994 by Stephen Arterburn

All rights reserved. Written permission must be secured from the publisher to use or reproduce any part of this book, except for brief quotations in critical reviews or articles.

Published in Nashville, Tennessee, by Thomas Nelson, Inc.

This book was originally published in hardcover by Thomas Nelson, Inc.

Fat goals for men and fat goals for women are reprinted by permission of PREVENTION. Copyright 1993 Rodale Press, Inc. All rights reserved.

Printed in the United States of America.

Library of Congress Cataloging-in-Publication Data

Arterburn, Stephen, 1953–
    Gentle eating / Stephen Arterburn, Vivian Lamphear, Mary
Ehemann.
        p.   cm.
    ISBN 0-8407-9700-1 (hardcover)
    ISBN 0-7852-7501-0 (mass market paperback)
    1. Reducing.   I. Lamphear, Vivian, 1954–   II. Ehemann,
Mary E., 1955–   .   III. Title.
RM222.2.A78   1994
613.2′5—dc20   93–33169
                                                                       CIP

8 9 10 11 12 13 14 15 — 02 01 00 99

To all those who have suffered or are suffering with a food addiction.

To Ken, Ryanna, and Dylan.

Contents

Preface

This book was developed by three people who have been successful at maintaining their weight loss for at least a decade. Although the approach presented has not been proven through research, it has been proven in their lives. Dr. Vivian S. Lamphear did much of the research that formed the clinical foundation for the approach that has worked for all three. Mary Ehemann did the work on the recipes found in Section 2 as well as provided ideas for the text. Stephen Arterburn wrote the book, and since much of it is about his personal experience in keeping sixty pounds off for over fifteen years, the book is written in his voice.

Please note that each chapter begins with the diary entry of a fellow struggler who has done battle with the issue being addressed.

The authors wish to thank the Nelson team who helped develop this life-changing program into a book:

Victor Oliver
Chuck Moore
Bruce Barbour
Bob Zaloba
Sara Fortenberry
Lila Empson

Introduction

Welcome to a journey that is designed to change your life from the inside out. Within the pages of this book is authentic hope for people who have struggled with their weight and have been unable to find any method of weight loss that would last for more than a few months or a year or two. It is a gentle plan, one that you can live with and one that will help you live. There is nothing hard or harsh within it. You have experienced too much of that. It is time you tried a more gentle, humane way of treating yourself and implementing change. Here you will find a tried and true plan with living examples of its effectiveness. Each coauthor has worked on this project from a perspective of personal experience with weight loss that has lasted for at least ten years and has been in excess of twenty-five pounds. This journey is for those who want to lose a lot for a long time— I hope for a lifetime.

If you are interested in losing five or ten pounds so you can fit into a swimsuit or have a picture taken or look good at a wedding, this book isn't for you. You are interested in a fast trip to instant results. You may lose weight, but there is about a 90 percent chance you will regain it. Every time I think of people doing something like that I remember a fancy wedding in Newport Beach where the full-size bride had lost fifty pounds for the ceremony. The couple hadn't been married thirty minutes before she was eating roast beef, chips, cheese, dips, candy, chocolate cake, and thousands of other calories and fat grams. She gained her weight back faster than she lost it, and now she is in worse shape than she was before. I wonder if that picture of her in her wedding dress is a pleasant memory or a source of irritating comparison? Wouldn't it have been great if she looked back at that wedding picture and realized that she had never been that overweight since then?

If you are losing weight to look good at an event, you may get a nice picture, but you may only be adding misery to your life. Most likely, you will show up with less weight, but a lot of what you will lose will be muscle. Then once you've proven to yourself and everyone else that you can hit your target, you'll most likely go back to your old eating patterns and gain back all the weight you lost. But you won't gain muscle. You'll regain fat. So if you want the quick fix that always has a bounce-back, weight-gain disaster at the end, you can find a way to lose the ten pounds for the picture or the event, but I don't think it's worth it. This plan is designed to prevent you from ever having to reduce like that again.

This plan is for all of us who are tired of the frustrating and self-defeating process that leaves us feeling worse about ourselves than when we started. It is for all of us who know that we can lose weight because over a lifetime we've lost about one thousand pounds. No, we don't need to prove our ability to lose it. We need help in how to never find it again. If that's you, you picked up the right book, and I believe it will be the last weight-loss book you will ever have to buy because this one is designed to last a lifetime.

Am I promising you results? No. The results are up to you and your ability to implement this plan. But I think you will be able to see very early on that this plan will provide you with the greatest hope for lasting results in the way you look and the way you feel about yourself. If you are like me, your excess weight has caused you to feel like a second-class person for too long. It has left you feeling inferior and often overlooked. You are ready to break through your weight barrier so others can finally see the real person who has been underneath all this time. Once you do that, some wonderful surprises and great moments are in store for you.

Before you begin this gentle journey, however, determine that you actually need it. Some people may feel overweight, but they are not. They measure themselves against an unrealistic standard. The problem is literally in their heads. The information below should help you sort out whether this is the book for you. First, look at an old weight standard published in 1959 by Metropolitan Life Insurance Company (see fig. I.1).

Height (without shoes)	Weight (without clothes)	
	Women	Men
5'0"	103–115	—
5'1"	106–118	111–122
5'2"	109–122	114–126
5'3"	112–126	117–129
5'4"	116–131	120–132
5'5"	120–135	123–136
5'6"	124–139	127–140
5'7"	128–143	131–145
5'8"	132–147	135–149
5'9"	136–151	139–153
5'10"	140–155	143–158
5'11"	—	147–163
6'0"	—	151–168
6'1"	—	155–173
6'2"	—	160–178
6'3"	—	165–183

FIGURE I.1. 1959 weight standards

It's a very tough standard to hit. There is nothing gentle about it. If you compare yourself to this old chart, you may be so overwhelmed by the amount of weight you have to lose just to get to the high end of your scale that you give up before you ever start. Apparently, there were many problems with this scale, and the government came up with a more realistic one in 1990 that is closer to what represents average weight. See how you compare in this scale (fig. I.2), and see how much more reasonable it is than the older one (fig. I.1).

Height	Weight	
	19–34 yrs.	35 yrs. +
5′0″	97–128	108–138
5′1″	101–132	111–143
5′2″	104–137	115–148
5′3″	107–141	119–152
5′4″	111–146	122–157
5′5″	114–150	126–162
5′6″	118–155	130–167
5′7″	121–160	134–172
5′8″	125–164	138–178
5′9″	129–169	142–183
5′10″	132–174	146–188
5′11″	136–179	151–194
6′0″	140–184	155–199
6′1″	144–189	159–205
6′2″	148–195	164–210
6′3″	152–200	168–216

FIGURE I.2. 1990 weight standards

An example of how tough the old chart can be is the case of a forty-year-old man who is five ten and weighs 170 pounds. Under the old standard, he would be considered 12 pounds overweight. Under the new standard, he would be 18 pounds from being considered overweight. A thirty-five-year-old woman who is five eight and weighs 160 pounds would be considered 13 pounds overweight by the old standard. The new standard would place her 18 pounds from being overweight. By working with the new chart, you may find that you don't have as far to go as you thought.

In addition to figuring out numerically if there is a problem, you need to address certain emotional issues that can help you discover if this journey is for you. Answer the following questions with your best attempt at revealing the truth about yourself.

1. Do you hate the way your body looks?
   ☐ yes ☐ no

2. Do you keep clothes in your closet that are too small in hopes of one day fitting in them, but you haven't been able to yet?
   ☐ yes ☐ no

3. Do you constantly compare yourself to others and try to figure out how much more or less they weigh than you?
   ☐ yes ☐ no

4. Do you ever eat so much that you feel you have to either throw up or take a laxative to get the food out of your system before the calories can affect your weight?
   ☐ yes ☐ no

5. Do you ever go on binges, and you eat from the time you get up to the time you go to sleep?
   ☐ yes ☐ no

6. After you eat, do you frequently experience tremendous amounts of guilt and shame?
   ☐ yes ☐ no

7. Have you literally lost hundreds of pounds through various diets but find you are unable to keep off the weight over an extended period of time?

☐ yes ☐ no

8. Are you at least twenty pounds overweight and unable to reduce to your desired weight?

☐ yes ☐ no

9. When you are anxious and under stress, do you find your food intake almost doubling?

☐ yes ☐ no

10. Have you found that the only way you can lose weight is to fast and starve yourself because once you start eating, you cannot stop?

☐ yes ☐ no

11. Has a physician ever told you that you needed to lose weight or you would experience a grave medical problem, such as high blood pressure, heart disease, diabetes, cancer, or some other illness?

☐ yes ☐ no

12. Do you feel that people reject you because you are so overweight?

☐ yes ☐ no

13. Do you consume mostly food that has been fried or contains a large quantity of sugar and fat?

☐ yes ☐ no

14. Do you get the impression that you often eat as a form of medicating some old wounds from your past?

☐ yes ☐ no

15. Do you have a hard time sleeping at night due to feeling bloated or having to get up frequently to go to the bathroom?

☐ yes ☐ no

16. Do you find that immediately after you decide not to eat anymore, you begin to obsess over food?
☐ yes ☐ no

17. Do you seem to have less and less control over your eating habits?
☐ yes ☐ no

18. Even in the midst of many adverse consequences from your weight, do you find it impossible to stop the out-of-control eating?
☐ yes ☐ no

19. Do you ever resort to diet pills to control your weight?
☐ yes ☐ no

20. After you have finished a meal, do you immediately start looking for something else to eat?
☐ yes ☐ no

If you answered at least three questions in the affirmative, there is a good chance you are on the right path and this is the right book for you. Remember it is for people who want long-term results and are willing to undertake some changes to keep their weight off for good.

Before you attempt any change in life-style, however, you need to start with a physical examination. Go to your doctor and have your heart and blood pressure checked; get blood work done. Perhaps you have high blood pressure or high levels of cholesterol. These factors are extremely important when selecting your food. Although some foods can be low calorie or low fat, they may contain high levels of cholesterol. Tell your doctor you want to change your weight, and ask for recommendations of proper foods for you.

This journey will radically change your life, the way you interact with others, and how you feel about yourself. This journey will allow you to experience the freedom you have always wanted—from the inside out. It's time to get started.

Section 1

THE GENTLE EATING PLAN

Chapter 1

The Beginnings of Change

People always told me I needed to lose a little weight. Losing wasn't the problem. I had lost hundreds of pounds on a thousand diets. No, the only problem with losing was that no matter how much weight I lost, I still felt like a loser. I could set a goal like the best of them, and I could achieve that goal. But it never lasted. Nothing in my life seems to last very long except one thing: hunger. Hunger is always around. It's there to remind me that although I feel it down deep in my stomach, most of my dissatisfaction is far beyond what goes on inside my body. My hunger is much more in my mind and in my soul. I long to be complete and feel complete. I hate feeling like a dumb, stupid loser.

I wonder why the rest of the world doesn't have to fight this battle? Why can so many others eat so much and never gain a pound or an inch? I wonder if God is punishing me for something I should have done or something I should not have done? I wonder if I am punishing myself? I wonder if perhaps I am the very culprit who has turned my body against myself? I wonder if I am my greatest enemy? I wonder if someday, somehow, I am going to set myself free and allow myself to finally achieve what I can? A hungry soul is a painful companion. I'm ready to fill it up with something better, something more meaningful than food that always begs for more to follow.

I wonder if I am at that place they call the bottom? Oh, God! I sure hope so. I don't want to go any farther down.
—A Fellow Struggler

REACHING DESPERATION

I was fed up! I was tired of feeling like a second-class human being. I wanted my life to be different. For once, I wanted to look in the mirror without feeling shame for the way I looked. I wanted to one day feel wonderful about myself and the body I inhabited. That was a feeling I had never experienced in all of my twenty-four years on this earth. But I was determined to win the weight battle. I dropped some weight the summer before my senior year in college, but it came back from time to time. I needed to lose more—forever. So on a cold winter day in Laguna Beach, California, I decided to re-create myself into a person who did not look fat in the eyes of everyone else and especially not in my eyes.

I was determined that whatever changes I made, they would last a lifetime. I had lost probably five hundred pounds over the years, but none of them stayed off. Each futile attempt at quick weight loss was punished by the recurring nightmare of out-of-control eating that showed up on the scales and in tight waistlines. Everything I had done was to find the quick fix and the instant solution. Each time I had clung to some new technique or fad diet, I had been able to produce immediate results but no lasting change. I wanted to do something that could change my life and lifestyle forever.

Like others who try to lose weight fast, I had made previous attempts that were nothing more than ego trips designed to get me looking good quickly for a picture or a short-term project. That day in Laguna Beach I had come to the end of myself. I was ready to go through the process of gradual but lasting change. I had never approached my weight from that perspective before. If I could pull it off, it would be the fulfillment of a long-term dream.

THE BEGINNINGS OF A NEW LIFE

I was involved in the psychiatric health care business. Fortunately for me, my first experiences were good ones, and I was moving up the corporate ladder of a leading psychiatric health care company. I needed to go where the business was, so I moved to California. It was the right decision. I did well with the company.

But the minute I arrived in California, I was confronted by culture shock. It seemed like everyone's body was well sculpted. My boss had found me an inexpensive bachelor's apartment on the beach, so I constantly saw trim southern Californians playing in the sand along the waters of the Pacific. With my overweight body, I did not look like I would ever fit in with my new community.

I decided that if I was to at least feel like I belonged, I must take off weight and gain new self-confidence. I did not want to be involved in the past rituals of weight loss that had left me with a temporary loss of bulk but a longer term gain in fat. I was unwilling to follow the advice I had accumulated from countless articles and books that guaranteed me a new life after an easy weight-loss scheme.

Since I was no longer into schemes, I decided to develop a plan that I knew could work for me. A gradual and gentle plan that would take into account the personality of someone who had been plagued by overeating. A plan that would provide any serious adherent with a body minus unneeded and unsightly body fat. I wanted to win at the weight game.

Until then, following the advice of everyone else, I had lost miserably.

CHANGING HOW I ATE, NOT WHAT I ATE

I was determined to go slow and take baby steps toward a totally new body. I wanted a gentle approach. I knew that deprivation wasn't the answer. I also knew that any radical change in what I ate would not last. So I decided to change how I ate rather than what I ate. I was used to driving home after work and stopping at a fast-food place for a quick meal so I could get home and do nothing. I hurried through the food; I never enjoyed it. I was hurrying for no reason.

Change your environment.

I realized I needed a change of atmosphere and attitude. So I found a restaurant in town that was quiet and played very pleasing music. This place is called Partner's Bistro. Eventually, I would meet my wife there, have my engagement party there, and celebrate a lot of anniversaries there. Needless to say, I am pleased with the place I picked. It has a view of the ocean, and the chef prepares the food like I want it.

I replaced a fast-food frenzy with a leisurely meal in a beautiful restaurant with a wonderful view, soft music, and a staff that treated me with dignity. I turned a daily ritual of low satisfaction into a treat to myself. I looked forward to it every day. And because the meal took longer, I felt more full on less or the same amount of food, and I had less time at home alone to accumulate unneeded calories from snacks.

You might be thinking that finding a restaurant is a strange first step on a weight-loss program. Well, it is. The emphasis is not on the restaurant, though; it is on the mind-set and the setting. I found a pleasant environment, but I could have created one just as easily. Whether you go out or stay in, the concept of eating in a pleasant, stress-free location is the beginning to changing your life through long-term weight loss. There's more later on this concept that has become the foundation of this weight-loss plan.

A SCHEDULE CHANGE

The next thing I did still did not involve changing the amount or substance of what I ate. It did involve another gentle change in the way I lived and the routine I carried out. I knew I would have to gradually increase the calories I burned. I had always been aware that I had a calorie problem, not really an eating problem. I consumed too many calories, or I burned too few. I was determined that before I consumed less, I would find a way to burn more. I also knew how frequently I had gone on fitness kicks and how quickly I had abandoned them, so I did not want to do anything too severe or too strenuous.

One time I signed up at an expensive weight-lifting establishment that I could not afford. I thought that if I made the investment, I would most likely force myself to follow up and pump the iron I felt I needed to pump. The first time I went there I was assigned a personal trainer who put me through about twenty weight-lifting exercises. Red faced and gasping for air, I did my best to impress the guy. Finally, I became so dizzy I had to go outside and sit on the curb so I wouldn't faint. The experience was very humiliating, and I wasted every dollar I spent on the membership because I never went back there again. This time I was going to go so slowly and gently that I could not fail.

Change your schedule.

I hit upon the idea of a schedule change. And the schedule I had to change was my morning one. After more than a decade of keeping my weight off, I would say for anyone who is serious about making a permanent change, you need to start with the amount of time you have in the morning between getting up and either leaving for work or beginning your work at home. I had always set my alarm so that I had only enough time to shower, get dressed, stop and grab a doughnut, and speed off to work. With my new determination, I wanted to break the cycle that I knew contributed to too many calories consumed and too few burned off.

You might expect that I immediately joined a health spa and awoke two hours earlier so I would have plenty of time to go and work out. You might have made such schedule changes either to punish yourself or to show someone else how serious you were about your plan. I didn't have anything to prove to anyone but myself. I didn't pay any costly initiation fee to a club I would use only as long as the guilt remained. I didn't set the alarm two hours earlier so that I would have no choice but to see the darkness and return to the womb of warm covers. I didn't go to extremes as I had many times before. Instead, I went for a gentle change that I could handle with ease. It has become the second step in the plan toward permanent weight loss.

I set my alarm thirty minutes earlier than usual. That time was my initial sacrifice. Anyone can get up thirty minutes earlier than usual, and I found that I adjusted readily to an extra thirty minutes of daylight. I didn't rise to don my tennis shoes and running shorts. I couldn't run anyway so that would have been completely self-defeating. Instead, I rose to do something I loved to do. I watched television.

I put no additional stress or pressure on myself to perform or live up to a commitment. The change was gentle enough that I could continue it until it became a part of my routine.

LEARN TO BURN

About two weeks into my new plan, getting up earlier and eating in a more comfortable setting turned out to be highlights of my day. You may not believe it, but those two things began the weight-loss process. I didn't lose much, but it was enough to encourage me to take the next step.

The next step involved increasing the calories that I burned. Instead of sitting in front of the television set, I got dressed and went out for a very pleasant stroll through the neighborhood. I read that if I walked thirty minutes, I could probably burn off an additional one hundred calories or so. It felt wonderful to be up and outside breathing clean, fresh air in a world that seemed like it had been freshly re-created the night before. If you have never experienced the morning, I highly recommend it.

It was a long time before I started to jog, but by the time I did, I felt great, and it was a very gradual adjustment to increase my activity level to a jog. I couldn't jog far, so I walked and jogged and walked some more. I just kept doing what felt good. Now I have completed my first marathon. I hesitate mentioning that because in the beginning I had no desire to run a marathon or to run at all. So don't back out just because the path I ran down eventually turned into a marathon.

When I started out, I didn't realize that there was a side benefit to morning exercise. I know now that I burned off the calories while walking and I also burned more calories the rest of the day. The early exercise increased my metabolism so that I obtained an extra burn of fuel throughout the day. No longer did three hundred calories mean the same to me. Because I was burning more calories, I felt that I was eating food with fewer calories.

Change your activities.

Needless to say, the walking caused me to lose more weight. I was motivated to continue with my plan. Eventually, I didn't even think about burning calories or losing weight. I just went through my enjoyable routine.

THE REST OF THE STORY

Gradually, I learned more and more about the food I was eating, and in stages I made more and more gentle changes. I never had a sudden weight loss; it was all gradual. Little by little, I changed the amount I weighed and the way I lived. Five feet, ten inches tall, at my heaviest I weighed 220 pounds, and that dropped to a solid 160. Losing weight has made so much difference in my outlook and my self-esteem. Others can't believe that I was ever truly fat. At times I still feel that way, but the little episodes of negativity don't last long.

The plan began with going to a restaurant in the evening and watching television in the morning, and it turned into a whole new way of living. Since I hit forty last year, I am at a stage in life when I am watching my contemporaries gain fifteen or twenty pounds. That isn't happening to me. I continue to weigh just about what I have for more than fifteen years.

You can achieve similar results through this plan. If you are ready, this journey just may be the greatest thing that will ever happen to you and those you love.

The Prayer of a Gentle Eater

God, help me move slowly and wait patiently for the results I know can be mine.

Give me strength and wisdom in time of doubt.

Help me persevere until I am who I want to be, until I am who You want me to be.

Chapter 2

Creating an Environment for Gentle Eating

―――――

What I love the most, I attack. But more than anything else I do, I attack food. Show me food and I will show you how to attack it and destroy it and hope that you have attacked so well and eaten so fast that perhaps your body hasn't noticed. But it always does. I attack because I am out of control.

—A Fellow Struggler

―――――

When you attack food, food attacks you. If you provoke it—grab it and yank it around and slam it down your throat—it will not take the abuse lightly. It will counterattack and demand that you show it the respect that it is entitled to receive from someone who spends so much time worshiping at the altar of calorie intake.

If you are like me, you have spent the majority of your life attacking the food you eat. You buy food fast, eat it in a hurry, and quickly look for the next tidbit. As a result, more and more food satisfies you less and less. Dining is not an enjoyable experience other than that for a few minutes, you fill up your stomach, which is more enjoyable than trying not to eat.

It is amazing that so many of us who love food have taken away the satisfying aspects of the eating experience. We have turned a quality experience into an exercise in the stuffing of quantity.

Plan *to relax and enjoy your meals.*

You deserve better. One of the finest gifts you can give yourself is an enjoyable eating experience. If for some reason due to work or other responsibilities there is no way to have three relaxing eating experiences, you may have to settle for two. Changing a habit of hurry-up eating for even one meal a day would be a change that could not only alter your life-style for the better but also alter the amount of weight you carry around.

With a little effort and planning, you can turn dining into a time of relaxation and enjoyment. Even if you are a construction worker who eats out of a lunch box, you can treat yourself to a wonderfully relaxing and enjoyable eating experience. And in so doing, you will be able to alter your weight without changing what you eat. It may sound too simple, but it is true. In the process of working toward a long-term weight loss, focusing on *how* you eat rather than on *what* you eat is more important initially.

You have probably focused on what you eat over and over again in dreadful diets and found that the end result is failure. You probably know it is unhealthy to compare yourself to others, especially since you will find others who eat much more than you do and weigh less. Perhaps they, too, know the secret I discovered that has enabled me to keep the weight off. Now of course I'm not saying you can change your environment and then eat eight banana splits and not gain weight. Quite the contrary. A calorie is a calorie, a fat gram is a fat gram, and a thousand of them stacked on thousands of them will cost you your figure. But if you look at how you eat before you focus on what you eat, you are much more likely not to want eight banana splits.

Set your mind before you set your table.

Beating yourself up emotionally is not going to get you where you want to go weightwise. Trying harder and striving to be stronger are not going to get you there, either. It is time that you quit putting yourself down and start putting yourself first. You have what it takes to eat differently, enjoy food more, and feel satisfied on less food without even trying to cut down on the amounts.

THE SET AND THE SETTING

Gentle eating begins with getting your mind set before your table is set. You make a decision to stop, slow down, and get caught up in the process of feeding your body needed nutrients and treating yourself to a satisfying experience that will fulfill you and leave you feeling better about yourself. I hope you are tired of never feeling that you can get enough to eat. If you are at that point, perhaps you are ready to look at how you eat and where you eat. If you are, I believe the approach will result in lasting positive change rather than the cycle of temporary hopes that prove to be false and long-term frustration with an ever-increasing waistline.

Many people with eating problems feel overwhelming hunger pangs because they have waited so long since the last meal. They have the idea that if they can wait until late in the day to start eating, they perhaps will escape the calorie deluge, even though they consume thousands of calories from the time they start eating until they go to bed. Although they are proving they have willpower, they are also increasing the amount of fat on the body. The metabolism is lowered, and the deprived body, fearing long-term hunger and deprivation, will attempt to store more fat. By cutting out food during the day, they experience a paradoxical effect that hurts rather than helps.

Tell yourself that you're worth the effort.

Others don't wait long periods of time; they respond immediately to the first little hint of hunger, as if they were giving in quickly to the manipulative cry of a two year old. Part of being a baby is crying, and there is no need to rush to stop the baby from being upset. Babies are survivors; you can actually take your time getting them changed or feeding them the food they want. The same is true about hunger. Tummies get hungry, and you don't have to respond so quickly. You are not going to die if you live with the feeling of hunger for ten or fifteen minutes. Many people with an excess of one hundred pounds feel they might starve if they don't get something to eat—*now*! So they race to find a substance that will stop the internal aching emptiness that reminds them that their lives are empty and that their souls feel empty, too. They want to feel anything but that emptiness, and they want it fast. They seek out fulfillment in the quickest form so they ingest a high-calorie, high-fat, high-sugar something that has been labeled food. But when they are finished, they are unsatisfied and a bit angry that after being hungry, they stuffed themselves with junk. Then come the guilt, shame, remorse, and promises that it will never happen again. They swear to themselves that next time will be different—but it never is.

To stop this deadly fat-producing cycle, you have to think and make a decision that will have long-term results for your well-being. You have to tell yourself that you are worth the sacrifice and the time it will take to rethink your eating habits. You are worth slowing down for. You can take control of every area of your life if you start with this one area of how you are refueling yourself to face the reality of your days. That means planning ahead. No procrastinating right up until mealtime is allowed. You have to develop a plan and carry it out. That plan must include what you will focus on while you eat and where you will eat. It means creating an environment that will lead to the most satisfaction possible from the least amount of food.

CREATING A SAFE ENVIRONMENT

There are definite things you can do to make your home a safe place and a positive environment in which to eat. If you are single, it will be easier. If you are married and have children who live on potato chips and colas, it will be more difficult; yet even with kids, it can work. If you do have a family, the first issue to resolve is whether or not you want the people you love to be living on potato chips and colas. To help yourself, you can start a revolution within your family that will change their eating habits forever. Removing the foods that give you the most problems is the first step in creating a supportive environment for long-term weight loss.

Compulsive overeating usually runs in the family, so you would do well to sit down and talk about it openly. Hold a family meeting or a meeting with your spouse. Discuss that family members can support each other in a plan for healthy eating. Even if your spouse does not struggle with compulsive overeating, explain that you need support. Together, draw up a list of foods that will be available all the time; include fresh fruits and vegetables and perhaps add low-salt pretzels, air-popped popcorn, and sugar-free cereal. Then prepare another list of foods that might be available only on weekends or special occasions: fat-free chocolate cake, fat-free yogurt, low-fat cookies.

Step 1: Create a safe eating environment and a new mental environment.

The goal in making your home safe is to remove unsafe high-calorie, high-sodium, high-fat foods. Fill your refrigerator with foods you'll find in the recipes in Section 2, "The Gentle Eating Cookbook." To further enhance your success, set up a regular time to meet each week and talk about the achievements you have made or perhaps the difficulties you have encountered.

PICKING THE PLACE

Where you eat has a lot to do with the satisfaction you derive from food. If you eat in a crummy place, you are likely to eat crummy food and feel crummy when you are finished. You will require more crummy food to reach a satisfaction point than if you were eating truly wonderful food in a wonderful place.

Consider these equations related to the amount of food ingested and the satisfaction it brings:

A lot of poorly prepared food + an unattractive
setting = low satisfaction

Enough good food + a pleasant
setting = high satisfaction

If these equations are correct, and I believe they are, you will get more satisfaction from less food by merely changing the environment in which you eat. You won't be depriving yourself; you will be eating as much food as it takes to feel satisfied, but the weight will come off because you will naturally want less food.

When I decided to make my big change that led to a new body, I started to eat in a nice restaurant. Most people in the diet industry would cringe at the suggestion that a good first step toward losing weight is eating out more. That can be the cause of many additional calories and substantial expense. But for me, it changed the lifelong habit of food slamming that almost always left me craving the next meal as soon as the last one was over.

I found that if I took the time to relax and look across the street to the ocean, my craving for food eased immediately. I started to feel satisfied even before I put the first bite in my mouth. By the time I was ready to order, I was able to think about salad or soup rather than pasta dripping with cheese or a piece of meat sautéed in butter. The environment and my mind-set allowed me to walk out of that restaurant having eaten much less and feeling much more satisfied with the food I ate and the person I was.

CREATING AN ENVIRONMENT OF PEACE AND BEAUTY

The act of choosing a nice environment over a fast-food place was key for me to make a long-term change in my weight. However, there are some problems with choosing a restaurant that I have tried to help you correct. The biggest problem is that restaurants are expensive. You are paying someone else to fix food you could fix, and you have to buy it at a premium price. If you eat at home, you will pay less for your food. The problem is that many people do not enjoy eating alone. The coauthors and I came up with an inexpensive way to radically alter your environment at home. It will enable you to increase the satisfaction quotient of your food without the expense of eating out.

We developed a video called *Gentle Thoughts for Gentle Eating* for you to watch while you eat. It has affirmations and beautiful music in the background of breathtaking scenes of nature's splendor. The price is less than the cost of a meal in a restaurant so it's paid for after only one meal. With this small investment, you can transform your home into a rest stop with a view of some spectacular places in the world.

If you have kids, you may want to feed them first, then enter a new environment with the video.

When you go to work, you may be able to use the video

for only one meal a day. If it is the evening meal, you won't be sleeping on so many unused calories because you'll eat less. Once you have viewed the video a few times, the scenes will stick in your mind. Then by playing only the audiotape (sold with the audio abridgment of this book), you will be able to mentally visualize the scenes.

I am inviting you to create an eating event. I am suggesting that you take yourself to a quiet world with beautiful scenery and relaxing music and encouragement to slow down and smell the carrots. The video will get you started with what to think about and how to pace yourself. Then you can take over and re-create that experience no matter where you are. You can always be in search of a new place to relax while you feed yourself nutritious and satisfying food.

GENTLE EATING

This change to a slower pace and a more comfortable setting is called gentle eating. You are being gentle with yourself and with your food. You are showing yourself and the food proper respect. You are canceling out all of your programmed thoughts about eating. Your focus will begin to shift away from mounds of food that you enjoy very little to a little less food that you will enjoy a lot. And you won't consciously have to change anything you eat. The changes will come naturally.

WHAT ABOUT FAMILY?

You may be thinking that you have four kids who are rowdy at the dinner table and there would be no hope for you to enjoy a meal as I suggest. If you are thinking that, you have a tremendous responsibility to your family to radically alter the way you eat together. Food habits are passed down from generation to generation. If you can go through the ordeal of helping them change now, they won't have to go through the ordeal you went through. They also won't have to carry around the weight you have had to carry around. You could create a transitional generation in your family just by making a decision to alter the environment of family meals.

Why not suggest that for a while, the whole family is going to treat itself to a new eating experience in the evening? Although there will be a few giggles at first, your family will most likely love the change. Suggest that the kids and your spouse get spruced up a bit for dinner—nothing formal, just no ratty old jeans and T-shirts covered with dirt from the day's activities.

Most important, when the family eats together turn off the television. No, don't skip this part. You need to turn off the television and turn on background music. It will encourage everyone to eat slower and enjoy the food more. You will probably want to lower the lights and light a few candles to make the table look extra special. In making these changes, you may be surprised to discover that your kids enjoy themselves, and they may ask to invite friends to dinner more often.

Create a transitional generation in your family.

Everyone enjoys being treated special. Making mealtime a special time will alter the amount of food it takes to satisfy the family and will encourage the art of conversation. If that reduces tension in the family and allows more good things to be expressed and love to be shared, the results are going to go far beyond improved waistlines.

The Prayer of a Gentle Eater

Dear God, I know I need to slow down and enjoy the gifts You have given me. I know I hurry to hurt myself. In the rush, Lord, remind me to stop and experience Your gentle love for me. Help me to find peace in the storm.

Chapter 3

Making Time for a Change

I love the night when all is dark and I am alone to do what I like without anyone to interfere. In the late night I have no judges to make me feel that I do not measure up. I have myself, and I have my pleasures of a thousand friends who join me in watching the illuminated tube. So the hours I sit here, I feed my heart and for a few moments feel some level of satisfaction. But I am never satisfied. I always need more. I always want more. Then my private ritual begins.

—A Fellow Struggler

TAKING A NEW PATH

At the point of desperation with my weight, I made one of the best decisions of my life. When I look back on it, I am still amazed that after years of decisions that only added to my problem, I finally made one that made good sense and got me started on a truly effective long-term weight-loss plan.

I didn't pick the health club route, and I didn't pick the deprivation and diet route. They had failed me before. Life was passing me by, and I wanted to finally become a part of it as a human being with my head up rather than always down in shame. All of those factors led me to decide to take a new path. I decided that it was a time for a change, and if it was going to be a real change with real results, I needed to make the time for change and take the time for change.

For years I had heard that if I wanted to lose weight and keep it off, I had to take in fewer calories or find a way to burn more. I had failed to find a way to take in less food, so I needed a way to burn more. My typical schedule was to sit up late watching Johnny Carson and eating at least two snacks after dinner. More often than not, my late night viewing turned into a progressive dinner. I usually progressed from something that was fairly healthy to a huge bowl of ice cream or something equally wonderful that I wanted in the first place.

No matter how much self-control I could show during the day, I lost it at night. I went to bed most of the time with a full stomach and empty emotions. Then I slept late, right up until the time I had to get up and dress for work. On weekends I stayed up even later only to rise even later. That made it even more difficult to get up on Monday morning.

The late hours always made me feel heavier. They seemed to sap my strength as well as the time my brain needed to replenish itself. When it was time to get up, I seemed to just be getting into the kind of sleep I needed. The warm bed was a very comfortable place to remove myself from. Some days I wouldn't. I would call in sick and sleep into the late morning. But when I did, it was as if I had crossed over some barrier and had slept too much. I felt very tired even after ten hours in bed. I just couldn't seem to get the sleeping part of my life right, and it affected every other part of my life. I wasn't me—at least that is what I told myself.

If you stay up late, eat in the wee hours, and are extremely tired the next morning, you have no time to exercise. Your schedule is highly distorted so that you are awake to add hundreds of additional calories and you are asleep when you could be burning off some of them in the morning. You want to lose weight, but everything you do—even your schedule—sets you up to stay overweight.

One of the best things you can do for yourself and your future is to alter your schedule so that you have less time to eat and more time to burn up a few calories.

Notice that the first step in becoming more active does not involve burning up more calories; it involves regulating your schedule. If you decide to start exercising immediately, you'll soon give it up because you'll be making two big changes—altering your schedule and exercising. So back off a little, relax, and figure out how you can get to bed thirty minutes or an hour earlier and get up thirty minutes or an hour earlier the next morning.

Step 2: Change your schedule to make time for exercise.

When I began the program, I set my alarm thirty minutes earlier, and when it went off, I did myself the favor of getting up, turning on the television, and making myself breakfast. I think the gradual changes built on a foundation of being gentle with myself have kept me with this plan so long.

LATE NIGHT TELEVISION

You may want to make this change, but you are reluctant to give up your late night programs that have become so much a part of your life. Giving up a favorite talk show or a wonderful series in reruns is like giving up an old friend. But you don't have to give up that old friend if you have a VCR—well, at least a VCR that you can program. Once again, you are not giving up something or depriving yourself of something you enjoy, other than some sleep. You're just making a minor adjustment to your schedule. That is a small achievable goal you can attain for yourself.

Turn off your TV a half hour earlier at night.

Often the habit of staying up to watch late night shows is an indicator of a much bigger problem than spending too much time in front of a tube. I know that when I become depressed, I do not sleep well, so I wander to the TV to pass the sleepless time. I usually make a stop or two by the refrigerator to satisfy a feeling of emptiness and what I perceive to be hunger. In reality I know that I am depressed, and I eat to make myself feel better.

Set your alarm for a half hour earlier in the morning.

I think that many people overeat to ease a deep and growing depression. I believe there are many like me who medicate themselves in the dark hours of the night with the dependable friend called food. Perhaps, like me, you have found food to be the most trusted substance on the face of the earth. It is always available, looks innocent, and seems to have a unique way of soothing whatever ails you. The more depressed you become, the greater your need to medicate the depression with delightful calorie-laden

foods that bring a short-term sense of fulfillment and satisfaction. The depression remains, however.

As you know by now, if the change is going to last, it is
going to have to be a change that's easy to implement and
easy to maintain. The change I recommend is that you find
a way to turn off the television thirty minutes earlier in the
evening and set the alarm thirty minutes earlier than usual.

CONSIDERING THE
BENEFITS OF CHANGE

Thinking through some of the great benefits of an extra
half hour in the morning may be helpful. As a person who
stays awake into the wee hours, you may be unable to
imagine much good about the morning, and you may also
wonder why anyone would want to be awake any sooner
than *absolutely* necessary. I understand your feelings, but
there are some other things to consider.

The morning can be a wonderful time when you use it to
lay the foundation for the rest of the day. You may be in the
habit of getting up, dressing, and grabbing whatever food is
available as you rush out the door to leap into your car and
start your daily routine. But one-half hour of extra time can
alter the entire course of your day. That extra thirty minutes
can make the biggest difference of your life. Let me explain
how.

When you first start this schedule change, you may want
to just watch television or read the paper until it is time to
get dressed for work. But eventually, you can use the time
to consider the tasks before you and set priorities. You can
use your half hour to think about some of the aches you
feel in your soul and what you will do to relieve them. I
hope you will use the time to develop a plan to succeed

with your life and then live out that plan. The important thing is that you cut out a half hour of wasted time at night and replace it with a half hour of productive, peaceful time in the morning.

There is something almost spiritual about the morning for me. The world seems clean and healed, and when I become a part of those early hours rather than race through them, I feel clean and healed, too. I find serenity in the morning before the world sets out on a tear. There is a quiet peace that cannot be experienced any other time of day. That quiet might be interrupted by a trash truck or an early morning bus, but it quickly returns to entice me to think of things beyond the desperate struggle to survive. Instead, I am called to think of who I am, why I am here. It is a great time to pick up a Bible or a book of devotions to discover a divine and eternal perspective on who I am and what I am to do.

If instead of making time for this spiritual retreat, you awake to a repeated hustle and bustle, if you never sit in the morning hours to contemplate purpose and meaning, it is no wonder that in the absence of these thoughts and experiences you must find a superficial peace in consuming food you do not need that produces results you do not want. Taking the time to make a change can break the cycle of meaningless living and reward you with a daily restoration of your soul. I believe that adjusting your schedule will change your life by laying a foundation for what is important rather than allowing yourself to become lost in the hurry-up routine of the world.

Change starts when you take time to change. You must develop a plan to change, and within that plan, you must find additional minutes that will add meaning and quality to your life. I challenge you to try it for ten days.

The Prayer of a Gentle Eater

Dear God, help me take time to ask for Your help. Help me find the time within my day to spend it with You. Wake up with me, walk with me, and guide me. Let this time together be a time for me to establish my priorities. Help me enjoy this day from beginning to end.

Chapter 4

Move It
to
Lose It

Every time I see an athletic shoe commercial with a lean body running or jumping, the pangs of guilt hit me. I want to be that person and experience the same freedom moving that fast and looking that good. I tell myself that I'm going to get started on a new program. I'm going to walk and run and work out and sweat it all off. But I know I won't. I hardly have enough energy to get up out of this chair and walk to the kitchen for another bag of chips. Maybe tomorrow will be different.

—A Fellow Struggler

THE EXTREMES
OF OVEREATING

There are a couple of common extremes among overeaters. The hyperactive overeater is on the move all the time, eating as she goes, with too much to do to stop and have a quality eating experience. It's almost as if food is a tranquilizer, but she can never get enough of the drug to calm herself down and relax. For this person, thinking about exercising more would almost cause a coronary. First of all, she would think there would be no way to be more active. Second, she would not be able to imagine fitting additional exercise into her schedule. She already has too much to do in too little time.

The other extreme is characterized by the overeater who is depressed and uses food as an antidepressant medication that needs to be administered almost around the clock. I lived the life of the depressed overeater, and I know just how difficult it is to move. Every cell in the body seems to weigh twice as much as it should, and there is often little motivation to walk across the room, much less to exercise.

I understand both extremes, and I know that for people at either extreme and for all those caught in the middle, exercise is not something easily incorporated into daily living.

REFUSING TO OVERDO IT

I'm sure there have been times in your life that you have finally made the commitment to exercise and you did it. In fact, you did it so well, exercised so intensely, that all the aches and pains you developed over the following days made you so uncomfortable that you needed more of your food drug to make yourself feel better. Then with all those aches and pains, there was no way you would consider exercising again. For one thing, you couldn't. It was too painful. I've been through that cycle a thousand times, and I know how helpless it makes you feel to attempt to increase your activity only to fail and end up eating more to cope with the frustration.

I invite you to take a much gentler approach with yourself. If you will, you will succeed, and you will feel like a success.

You will be able to increase your activity level so that you can achieve the weight that's within the accepted range for your age and height.

Be gentle, take your time, and enjoy the gradual steps you are taking to ensure that your body runs smoothly and efficiently and eventually weighs less. To do that, you have to rethink your strategy so that short-term failures can be replaced by long-term success.

If you have made an adjustment in your schedule and have been able to maintain that altered schedule, you have at least thirty minutes a day that you can use to work for you. You can do anything you want to with that time. Decide that you will not use it to sabotage yourself, inflict pain on yourself, or attempt something you can't do, setting yourself up for guaranteed failure. I recommend that you begin a gentle program of exercise and increased calorie burning by walking.

THE HEALING WALK

You can turn the time you walk into a gratifying time. Find someone to walk with you. By forming a partnership, you can encourage each other. Every morning when I run, I see two women in the neighborhood who meet at the same time and walk all over town. Their early morning laughter indicates they enjoy each other a lot.

One of our problems as overeaters is that we internalize our feelings. Rather than express them, we hold them in and bury them until they can no longer stay down. We try to smother them with food or feed their pain. Somehow we didn't learn how to process how we felt.

Another problem is that we are reluctant to be who we are. We are always trying to impress others. We often think that if we ever stop faking it, we will collapse and fall apart. We spend our lives acting out what others expect us to be and cram who we really are inside the smallest space of our existence. It is no fun, but we don't know any other way to exist. It has become second nature to us.

Step 3: Exercise gently.

Walking with a partner is a nonthreatening way to begin to reclaim the real and wonderful person you are. It is a means to practice the art of honest communication with another. Your partner can be the link back to who you want to be. As you spend day after day walking alongside your partner, you'll feel less and less need to put on a show or maintain a facade. Eventually, you will reveal hurts and hopes. One morning you will walk back in your house feeling great about the walk and feeling greater about the fact that you are finally letting another person know who you really are.

Several years after I began my early morning walks, I started training to run my first marathon. Just saying the words *first marathon* is amazing for me. You have to picture a guy who was once sixty pounds overweight, smoked two packs of cigarettes a day, and ate the most fat-filled, sugar-laden food in the world to understand how remarkable it was that I was able to run a block, much less run 26.2 miles.

While I was training for that marathon in Big Sur, California, I hooked up with two great friends, Margaret and John

Snyder. We ran together every Saturday on our training runs, and eventually, all of us finished the marathon together. The more we ran together, the deeper our friendship grew. We shared our struggles; we were open with each other. The runs went far beyond the physical and far beyond the emotional and moved into the spiritual. We would run along and pray for each other and pray that our problems would lessen and our wisdom would increase. Those were wonderful times that I will never forget.

You can have a similar experience if you are willing to take a risk and ask someone to walk alongside you and become a partner for thirty minutes a day. What a great excuse to develop a relationship!

I believe that people who truly need therapy should get it, but thousands of people paying thousands of dollars for therapy just need someone to talk to. Often therapists encourage people to talk things out and, in the process, work things out in their own minds. Therapists have more questions than answers. The right partner for a morning walk can save thousands of dollars in therapy.

If you prefer the solitude or if no one is willing to get up early to walk with you, you can always walk alone. You might want to get a radio/cassette player with a headset. It's not the same as having a growing friendship, but you can catch up on music tapes or listen to books on tape.

It's not an accident that the benefits of walking I've presented so far have been those outside the physical realm. When you do yourself the favor of starting to move, the benefits always transcend the easily identifiable fact that you are burning up more calories. But of course, there is a very definite physical benefit. You are going to breathe in more oxygen, and oxygen is vital to burning anything. You are going to expend energy and burn calories. A general rule is that for every mile you walk, figure on burning one hundred calories.

At a moderate pace, you should be able to walk two miles in thirty minutes, allowing you to lose conservatively about one pound every twenty days if you didn't take in more excess calories. Exercise tends to increase the appetite so you will have to be careful that you don't eat up all the physical benefits you have gained. When your appetite increases, don't panic. After your body understands you are not going to overwork it, the desire for food will return to normal. Walking thirty minutes a day for one year could result in a weight loss of almost twenty pounds if you did nothing else. I think you will enjoy walking so much that even if you did not alter one ounce of food consumption, three years from now you could end up with about sixty fewer pounds of fat and about one hundred more pounds of self-confidence and pure joy for living.

Boost your self-confidence by exercising.

I told myself a lot of reasons that I could not exercise. I put up hundreds of barriers between me and the act of getting my body moving. When I broke through all the excuses and started to move and breathe, I felt I had accomplished something spectacular. That good feeling and attitude boosted my self-confidence and motivated me to do more and want more for myself and my future. Walking was a turning point in my life. I hope it will be the same for you.

BEYOND WALKING

In time, you will want to add something extra to your walking routine. I made the mistake of going from walking to running. That was great for my cardiovascular fitness and for my lower body. But it was an unbalanced program. I needed to do upper body strength building. I eventually started lifting a few weights and doing some push-ups and sit-ups and whatever else I could think of to tone my upper body. I really felt a difference.

You may not want to use weights. A low-impact aerobics class that makes you move and stretch every part of your body can work just as well. If you incorporate some weights into the routine, you will achieve the same results as the mild weight-lifting program I started. The main thing is to lower your weight while you gradually give yourself new muscles. When you start to feel that you are growing in strength, you will feel great.

Gentle, gradual increases in exercise burn off the fat. Go too fast and you will crash and burn. If you can ease into your program, never getting too tired or too sore, you will have a greater chance of continuing to increase your fitness level. I know you want to feel what it is like to be in good condition. I know you want to do away with labored breathing. I know you want to feel the freedom to play tennis or volleyball or take an afternoon jog. It won't happen quickly. You will have to move when you would rather sit, but once you begin, if you go gently on yourself, you won't turn back. You will wonder why you waited so long to get moving.

The Prayer of a Gentle Eater

Dear God, I haven't done so well with what You have given me. I'm ready to move, and I'm ready to lose. Help me make it last. I want to look like a new person, feel like a new person, and act like a new person. Let's get going together.

Chapter 5

Developing Thoughts of a Winner

Today I tried to change. I failed. I thought I could do it. I was wrong again; for the zillionth time I was wrong. I just can't do it, and I never will. Dear God, I would give anything to be free from this hulking weight that drags me down as I drag it around. Why have I been cursed to live inside this body? Why do I have to be such a big loser? Oh, well, just keep smiling, look happy, and maybe it will be better someday.

—A Fellow Struggler

LEANING TOWARD NEGATIVE THINKING

It was almost automatic with me. Given the choice between a positive and a negative thought, I seemed to almost always slip into the negative. I tried to rationalize it away: I was so reality based that it was hard for me to see all the pretty and nice things others seemed to have no problem noticing. I called it my slant on life, but through the years, it became an attitude problem that permeated everything I did. It was a reflection of just how negatively I viewed myself.

If you are like I was, you will have to find a way to be

gentler with yourself. You will have to re-create an attitude that works for you and not against you.

When I was in the midst of struggling with my eating problem, I allowed everything to be a potential negative influence on the way I thought, felt, and behaved. I had all the wrong ideas about food. For instance, I viewed hunger as the enemy. Every time the least little pang occurred I thought I was going to lose control, or I envisioned putting on another ten pounds. It took time, but I finally realized how destructive those thoughts were. I understood that each thought had power, and the power I was creating was negative and destructive. I came to understand that my mind was my biggest enemy, and it had to be brought under control before my weight could be brought under control. Little by little, I began to stop the negative and move it into a more positive mode. It was a turning point not only for my weight but also for my attitude.

STOPPING THE NEGATIVE FLOW

If you are prone to see the downside, you must stop yourself in the midst of the negative and destructive ideas. I became an observer of my mind. I tried to evaluate what I said and thought. When I got off on a negative tangent, I would create a big stop sign in my mind. That big red sign would cause me to stop the negative flow of cynical and self-deprecating thoughts, feelings, and comments. It worked in allowing me to disrupt what would usually be a train of thought that left me feeling badly about myself and wanting to find relief from those feelings in the food I ate.

It was not an instant process, and it took much practice. I had learned negativity well. My mother taught me the art of worrying, and I was a dedicated student. To this day, I am reluctant to give up my worries and trust God to do what is far beyond my control. If you lived in a home where worry and negative comments were the norm, you will have to put up the dams that stop the negative flow. But you can do it if you will practice and never give up.

Once I stopped the flow of mental garbage, I needed to replace it with something positive and meaningful. So whenever the stop sign went up, I quickly replaced the glaring red sign with a glowing neon light that read, "You are worth it." I don't know why I came up with those exact words, but they helped me mentally elevate myself from a second-class heavy to a first-class equal to the rest of the world who deserved to make some painful sacrifices so that I would feel better about myself. Thinking about being worth it allowed me to focus beyond the current moment and see that each new bite I took only increased my problem later on. I realized that if I could replace a negative thought with a stop sign and a stop sign with a neon sign, I could also say no to food I did not need.

Step 4: Think like a winner.

I began to think of everything in a much different light. Even my view of family history began to change. My father has four brothers, and all but one is on the heavy side. Much of our family gatherings centered on food, and I was like all the rest of them lined up to get my share. I thought that my heritage had to be my destiny. But I started to challenge that thought. I started to believe that I could be different. I started to tell myself that rather than reproduce the problems of the past, I could resolve the issues concerning my eating habits.

I stopped thinking of hunger as a big brass alarm bell that went off in my head, signaling that if I did not eat something fast, I would become ill, get a headache, or impair my mental abilities. When hunger hit, I refused to let it control me. Eventually, I was able to think of hunger as an invitation to do something good for myself. Hunger became an invitation to eat something nutritious that would satisfy me. That thought change reduced my anxiety level and thus my urge to eat more than I needed. It was a very long journey for me to make that switch. Once I made it, however, I was able to alter my thinking in other more positive ways.

One problem area can control other areas of your life. A negative attitude about food affects relationships and work or school. But when you start to change one area, the other areas are affected, also. That is why I recommend that if people are struggling with their weight, they should also be working on the other problem areas of their lives at the same time. How do you view your relationships? How do you view God? How do you view your purpose in life? Think on these things. Allow yourself to re-create attitudes in all areas, not just food. As you do, you will find that the battles with food attitudes will be much easier.

DEGREES OF HUNGER

I started thinking about food and hunger like I started thinking about the other areas of my life. I avoided the extremes of all good or all bad. I stopped the black-and-white thinking. I began to consider more than whether or not I was hungry; I tried to determine how hungry I was. I always thought hunger was hunger, but I soon discovered that if I stopped to feel what was really there, hunger was not always the same sensation for me. Being hungry at 3:00 P.M. after having a great lunch was not the same as being hungry after spending several hours in the mountains with no food.

My old way of thinking almost set off a panic attack in my head that indicated I might die if I didn't find some food immediately. So I did something about that. I came up with hunger ratings: a rating of one hundred meant I was ravenous, and a rating of one meant I was satisfied, as if I just had a wonderful meal. Then when I got hungry, I stopped to rate it. Was I at fifty-five, or was I moving toward seventy? If I was at thirty, I would tell myself a pretzel would do. If I was at seventy, it was time to eat something more substantial. I was developing hunger responses other than the one I had, which was "stuff yourself whenever hunger presents itself." The more I relied on my ratings, the more food became a substance to satisfy hunger rather than something to calm my emotions or medicate my pain. And the more I evaluated my hunger, the more I was able to differentiate hunger from loneliness, depression, or fear. All of that came about by changing the way I thought.

When you start thinking positively about the signals your body gives you, you can use your brain to become your best weight-loss guide. By continuing to rethink what hunger means, you can move into eating just about anything you want because you become so good at choosing the appropriate size of the portions. I don't ever go into an ice-cream place and order three dips of ice cream. I used to. Now if I want ice cream, I order a small cone. And sometimes I throw half of it in the trash. I used to think that since I paid for it, I better eat it. Now I think that since I paid for it and it is mine, I might as well throw it away if I don't need all of it to satisfy myself.

Hunger evaluation has led to proper portion control of all foods. I can sit down at a table to eat, and before I fill my plate, I evaluate my hunger. I end up with much less food and feel much more satisfied once I finish the portions I choose.

Another area where my mind made a difference related to exercise. When I first started to exercise, my appetite increased. I panicked and thought that must mean I was going to go out of control. Thoughts of failure crept in. My situation seemed hopeless so I gave in to eating.

As I started to think differently, I was able to see that my appetite would naturally increase with activity and that a few extra calories to satisfy me were nothing compared to all I was burning off from the exercise. I persevered with the exercise, making sure that the time I exercised allowed me to burn off any excess calories.

My appetite began to return to normal, but when it did increase a bit, I didn't overreact. I was also able to make a decision about when I should reward myself with some of the more fattening foods I loved the best. Those rewards kept me motivated to earn them. With a change in attitude, I was able to eat the food I needed and from time to time reward myself with the food I wanted. This ability to change attitude enabled me to lose weight and keep it off over the long term. You, too, can accomplish your goal by following these guidelines!

THE POWER OF AN ATTITUDE

You may have an attitude or a thought problem like I did. You may tend to be negative whenever you have an option.

You may see things through black-tinted glasses. You may also be extremely irritated every time you encounter someone who seems to be having a great time at living. If you are like me, you can help yourself by changing your thoughts from self-destructive traps into self-productive guides toward the future you want. Your mind can become the trailblazer through the swamp of confusion and lead you into a completely new existence that you never dreamed possible.

It is no accident that so many people have written so much on the power of our thoughts to affect our behavior and the attainment of our goals. Whether it is positive or possibility thinking, some people have already figured out that this computer called the brain can be programmed to help us or to hurt us, and some of us are very good at programming that computer to do self-destructive programs. But once we crack the code and reprogram our brains to work for us rather than against us, we are truly on the road to total and complete life-style change, including body style.

Stop and think of all of the things going through your head that sabotage your potential and return you to old patterns and routines that you have proved over and over again to be counterproductive. Do you allow these thoughts to creep in?

- *I'll be this way forever.*
- *Nothing can help me.*
- *I've tried everything.*
- *I was just born fat, and I'll die fat.*
- *What's the use? Life is miserable and who wants to prolong the agony?*
- *I'm a loser.*

If you have been thinking anything close to these thoughts, it is no wonder that you continue to have a weight problem. The most powerful tool you can use to change how you feel and what you do is the brain. If you call up only statements of self-defeat, you will play out the defeat upon which you obsess. You end up having much more of a brain problem than a weight problem, and if you are to have any hope for controlling your weight, it will begin with your brain. You *can* reprogram your brain to help you win the weight battle and conquer your doubts.

I can almost be assured of one thing about your thoughts regarding yourself: you have been too hard on yourself. Most people with a weight problem are victims of their own emotional abuse. They think things that are so negative that they make themselves emotional wrecks while they undermine their best intentions. You must realize that all those negative thoughts have gotten you nowhere. You must start being gentler with yourself.

DYING TO SELF

Dying doesn't sound too gentle. Death is about as harsh as you can get—especially if you have to put yourself through it. But I have found that one of the best things you can do for yourself is to literally kill a destructive thought or temptation to achieve the goals you have set for yourself.

Delay gratification.

Let me explain what I mean by dying to self. Let's say you are on a trip. You are determined that you will get back from the trip weighing less than when you started. To do that, you tell yourself that you will delay some instant gratification, that you will die to your instant desire for fulfillment to achieve a longer lasting goal.

Just as you sit down on the plane, secure in your resolve to make wise decisions about your weight, along comes a flight attendant who puts two sacks of peanuts on your tray. She is gone before you can request that the salty, oily, crunchy little fat producers be removed. Now you have a choice: satisfy yourself or die to self.

In those very tough moments of temptation, I take a deep breath and tell myself that I am not going to be beaten by my desires. I kill the thought of instant gratification. I delay the satisfaction. I visualize a pair of pants fitting loosely by the end of the vacation. I refuse to give in to my inclination to immediately satisfy every desire or wish. I determine that I will control my appetite and I will not allow my appetite to control me. I can win by allowing the feeling of hunger to be transformed into a victorious feeling of self-sacrifice and self-control.

As I push away those tempting little nuts, I breathe in a feeling of pride that I can conquer my immediate desires for the long-term goal of satisfaction with a fit body. In an instant, I choose pride over shame, and in that decision, I provide myself with the gentle assurance that I can be different forever. The more I win at this process, the easier it becomes because each day is another exercise in reprogramming the most important weight-loss tool I possess, my brain.

REPROGRAM YOUR BRAIN

In addition to choosing to delay your gratification, I invite you to gently mold your behavior with gentler thoughts about yourself and your potential. You really do become what you think about, and if you can change your attitude from failure to success, you are going to surprise yourself with results that have eluded you before. I urge you to work hard on this area that controls your life and the outcome of your attempts to weigh what you should in accordance with the range on the chart for your height and age. As tough as it is to say it or think it, you can have a thinner body.

There are a lot of ways to reprogram your thinking computer. Probably the easiest way to snap out of the negative mode is to memorize positive statements about yourself and then repeat them to yourself. So much of self-talk is so negative that even the least emphasis on the positive can produce a dramatic change in attitudes and actions. The following are some statements to replace the negative self-talk that has interfered with your efforts:

- I can do it.
- I don't have to repeat the past.
- I can look good.
- It's never too late to change.
- There is hope for me.
- There really is a thinner person living inside me.
- I am worth the effort.
- Change is never painless, and I can endure pain.
- I can control what I eat.
- Once I get started on a project, the options seem limitless about what I have the potential to do.
- I can become whoever and whatever I want to become.

Repeating these statements will carve out the negative comments you tell yourself and leave you with fairly positive thoughts about yourself and your future as a person of average weight. Finding evidence against the negative, distorted thoughts will also have a powerful effect on your thinking patterns.

Another exercise that will help you get your brain on your team for long-term weight loss involves thinking about a goal or a dream that you know would be possible if you were successful in losing weight. As I mentioned earlier, the only other time I was able to take off a substantial amount of weight was just before my senior year of college. I was at my maximum weight that summer in Waco, Texas, where I chose to work rather than go home. I was miserable, and I ate a lot of high-fat food like Mexican food to soothe my aching soul. I was smoking and overeating and not exercising, and there were plenty of reasons that I could have given up on becoming a thinner person. But I didn't.

I used my brain to motivate myself toward change. If you are overweight, you will understand my motivation. One of my goals was to be able to run with my shirt off and not be embarrassed. That to me would be the ultimate freedom. That goal initially started at Baylor. I would picture myself running down the street with the body of a muscular runner. It helped me stay motivated. I didn't lose all the weight I needed to or wanted to, but I did make some progress that stayed with me.

To further use my mind to motivate my actions, I pictured being able to sit around the swimming pool with my friends without being embarrassed to wear swim trunks. As I ran and worked out with exercise of all sorts, I kept that vision in my mind. That image and the positive self-talk helped me persevere in the daily routine.

From that experience, I recommend that you picture yourself doing something you don't like to do because you are overweight. Picture yourself doing that at an average weight. Or picture something you believe might happen if you weighed less. If you think you might have a greater chance of getting married, picture someone proposing to you. Once you find the picture that will motivate you, don't give it up until you achieve your goal.

RE-CREATING WITH THE CREATOR

If you think negatively about yourself, you may think that God has the same opinion. Let me challenge that thought with reality: God created you and loves you more than you could ever know. He wants the best for you and will help you have the best as long as it is in keeping with His greater plan. In reprogramming your mind, spend time with the God who made your mind.

Pray, meditate, and ask God to help you succeed. Tell God you want to fall back in His arms and trust your life to His will. If you are truly able to do that, your fears and anxieties can melt away. You may be startled to discover how comfortable life can be when you ask God to help you do what you can and ask God to go beyond and help you do what you cannot.

If I could convince you of no other thing in this book, it would be to change your mind about God. God is on your side. He loves you and seeks to see you succeed. Think upon that; let it saturate your mind. Begin to feel how God can satisfy your desires in a way that food never has—and never will.

CONCLUSION

Re-creating yourself begins with re-creating your mind. Your thoughts drive your feelings and your behavior. Before you work on how you feel or what you do, you need to fix the big thinker. It has been destroying all of your best intentions. Get your brain working with you rather than against you. Don't expect too much too soon. Be easy on yourself. Gradually, you will find that you really are in control. You really do have the ability to change your mind and change your thinking into that of a winner.

The Prayer of a Gentle Eater

Dear God, You have given me an amazing brain. I've spent most of my life using it to hurt myself, and now I want to use it to help myself. Help me stop the urge to give in to every desire or temptation. Give me courage to die today so that a new me can live the rest of my life. As I look back, God, I have failed myself many times, but You have never failed me. Give me what I need to be a new creature. Help me help myself to a new mind and a new spirit. I want to fill my mind and heart and soul with pictures that You would have me see. Fill my mind with Your thoughts of what I can be. Fill my mind with the potential found in Your love.

Chapter 6

Changing the Feelings Behind the Feedings

The world keeps spinning, the people keep running, and I sit here feeling left behind. All I have is myself and my wounds that I didn't ask for but I guess I somehow deserved. So I sit here in front of a TV that yaks and yaks and yaks to drown out the thoughts, the memories, the horror of just being me. And of course, I eat. I eat because for a moment, that wound feels a little better. If the world is going to neglect me, I will not neglect myself. Maybe I eat to punish the person who got wounded. If it's not the wounds, it's the fear. I face it every day. I get so anxious and uptight—as if the worst thing that could possibly happen is about to. Does anyone else feel so afraid? Do others feel safe? I wish the food could finally heal the fear.

—A Fellow Struggler

TREATING OURSELVES UNKINDLY

For many of us, life would be wonderful if it didn't hurt so much. If it weren't such an emotional struggle, we could do what we want and achieve some of the things we want to accomplish. We want so much to achieve a total change in the way we look, but most often the thing that gets in the way is the way we feel. All of us who are battling our weight are actually battling our emotions. They become our enemies of self-destruction that rob us of the opportunity to make good decisions leading to our goals.

Step 5: Change the feelings behind the feedings.

We are so hard on ourselves, so demanding of things beyond what we can reasonably expect to do and be. Few people have been gentle with us, and we follow their lead and beat ourselves up on the inside. If we are ever to make a change, we have to be gentler with ourselves. We have to treat ourselves emotionally as we want others to treat us. If we can finally be gentle with ourselves, others may be gentle, also. And we may find less reason to soothe our wounds with the needed medication of fat-saturated, sugar-soaked food.

FOOD FOR FEELINGS

In the arena of feelings, two types of eaters have a big problem in controlling their intake. The first is the depressed eater. The depressed eater feels badly about herself and the entire world in general. She sees little hope in getting out of her current dilemma, and she sees little hope in the long-term resolution of problems. She feels sad and trapped, and she eats to comfort herself. Essentially, she caters her pity party with food that produces so much excess fat that she cannot help gaining weight. Almost every overeater slips into this mode at some time when food is used as an upper.

The other type is the anxious eater. The anxious eater is uptight, worried, and concerned about things beyond his control. He is the savior to anyone who is in need. He neglects personal needs and compensates by fueling himself with massive quantities of food. Food is his tranquilizer, and he takes that tranquilizer so much that he overdoses on it. When there is nothing better to do, he eats, and there is rarely anything better to do. He is afraid of what might be and what might never be. He feels inferior to the rest of the world and is afraid the world will pass him by or cause him more pain than he has already known. In his insecure misery, he believes no place is safe; gloom and doom may be just around the corner.

Of course, the anxious eater is not always aware of all the things he is anxious over. He probably would not consider anxiety a big problem. He wouldn't relate to the word *fear*. He might say that he is a bit nervous. He might identify a pattern of being nervous and always picking up some food to either calm himself down or have something to do. Few overeaters stop eating long enough to examine what is behind this condition of nervousness. When they do, they find the fear.

You may eat when you are sad, or you may eat when you are anxious. If you are like many, you may eat in both circumstances. Your moods change quickly, and as you vacillate between the highs and lows, you pick up food to help you along the way. Whatever your mood or circumstance, you find comfort in food and seek it out as your drug of choice. You know there has to be a better way that will not trap you in a body that you deplore. You have not found that way. You want to find it and you have searched in many places for it, but a better way has eluded you. I hope you are finally finding it here.

WOUNDS

One reason we have a hard time finding a better way is that we have so many untreated wounds. They go untreated because they are painful to treat in a way that resolves them. Rather than resolve them, we continue to be controlled by them, and we attempt to medicate them.

I recently gave a seminar on dealing with wounds. I discussed the fact that we all had them, some worse than others. People in the audience took turns discussing their wounds and how they felt. One man talked of his anger toward his mother. She had passed him off to friends when he was six months old so she could live with a man who didn't want children and she could drink without the responsibility of her child. Because of his hatred of his mother and the bitterness toward his inability to overcome the hurt and get on with his life, he ate.

It was a moving discussion that ended with his visualizing his mother as a victim of her mother, who had abandoned her and left her to live without knowing how to love. I believe that everyone in the room was moved by the story and was able to relate personal experiences to the man's being trapped inside his cage of emotions. All of the years of hurt weren't healed, but he looked at his pain in a new way. As the tears rolled down his cheeks, a glimmer of hope started to shine in his eyes.

I expected that others, motivated by the experience, would open up and share their hearts in a desire to move toward an emotional breakthrough and change. I was mistaken. Seated a few rows from the front was a woman who was at least one hundred pounds overweight. She had a very simple question: "What if you don't want to change?" The woman revealed a life of abuse and pain that left her alone and hurting; food was her only companion. She knew she was in trouble, knew there was a better way, but she was too tired and unwilling to go through the process of change. She wanted to know if I had any advice for her.

I think that woman was like most of us, only she was a bit more honest than we are. We often act as if we want to change and feel better, but if we could truly be open and honest with ourselves, we would find that we are too tired to go through the pain of change. We are often overwhelmed at the mere prospect of it, our actions prove that we are uninterested in long-term change.

If that is where you are, there is hope. You can find emotional healing that will lead to a long-term change if you are willing to do one thing. It is the one thing that I encouraged the woman to do.

MAKING A CONNECTION

When you are stuck, and that woman was stuck, you need help to get unstuck. When you are unwilling to be the agent of change and motivation, you need to invite someone else into your life to motivate you to change. If you are willing to seek out another human being for the sole purpose to encourage you, you may be able to unlock yourself from self-destructive behavior. Alone, you may never break out of some of your most destructive cycles. With the encouragement of another, however, it may not be as hard as you think.

You can turn to many sources to find emotional support. One of the first places to look is in a church. Tell the pastor you need to make some changes, but your cup is so empty that there is nothing left within you to make the changes. Tell the pastor you need someone to provide an emotional salve. Explain that you need a kind and gentle person to build you up and motivate you.

Or you may prefer a support group for codependents or, better yet, Overeaters Anonymous. Explain your need for a positive injection of emotional support. If the group doesn't have someone, try another group until you meet someone willing to invest time in your needy soul.

Or you may prefer to go to a therapist or a counselor. Many people consider seeking professional help an expensive admission of weakness, but I see it as a sign of strength. First of all, you can find counseling to fit your budget. Plenty of sliding-scale counseling centers will take what you can afford to pay. Second, people who seek counseling are not the weak; they are the strong who come to grips with the reality that they cannot in and of themselves acquire the skills needed to live life with meaning and purpose, free of damaging compulsions. A step into a counselor's office is a step up, not down. It may be the most vital step you can take in the process of healing out-of-control emotions.

If you need help finding a counselor or you believe your problem is severe enough to require treatment in a treatment center, call 1-800-NEW-LIFE.

EMOTIONAL PAIN

Emotional pain is never easy to reckon with. It is made even more difficult by our push-button, quick-fix society that demands we find an easy way and a fast way to resolve everything.

Emotional trauma has never been something that is quickly overcome. To cope with it, a person must undertake a journey of learning and healing. It is often a painful journey, but that pain never exceeds the severity of pain that builds up when a person refuses to resolve the negative emotions gathered in the soul. A person who has been abused and neglected will always be reluctant to face more pain.

You want the pain to be over. Somehow you have to reach the point where you can almost feel the reward of dealing with the painful side of your life. That is when you realize you have to walk back through some of the original pain to walk out of it forever. That is what frees you from the compulsion to eat.

Until the emotions are brought under control, you will probably not experience long-term success in keeping weight off. Out-of-control emotions cannot control the impulse that triggers the desire for unneeded food. If that impulse cannot be controlled, your best intentions will be derailed into failure every time there is an opportunity to eat. Once emotional control is regained, you can make a plan of what you want to eat and what you need to eat and then stick to the plan—no matter how many opportunities you have to gorge yourself. It does not occur overnight. It is a gradual shift into a different way of reacting to emotional discomfort.

Find a friend who can help.

This gradual change has tremendous benefits. I think overeaters are never more proud than when they shift into being able to say no, stick to a healthy eating plan, and not deviate from the course they have set. For many, their pain is so great they could not imagine having that kind of control over what they do.

THE TOUGH PART

Anyone I have known who was extremely overweight had emotional pain that needed to be resolved and tears that needed to be shed. The tough part is realizing that is you and realizing your need to get started. You require the maturity of a responsible person who can delay gratification long enough to get in touch with the issues driving you out of control. You may not be ready right now, but a gentle friend somewhere is ready to help you. Making that connection will be a step toward freeing yourself from the pain.

The Prayer of a Gentle Eater

Dear God, You know I have pain. And You know I don't want to feel it or relive it. You also know I need to. Please help me face the truth about myself. Help me be brave enough to face it. But first, God, help me be humble enough to find someone who will help me deal with the truth and the pain. Help me ask for help.

Chapter 7

Deprivation

Sacrifice, sacrifice, sacrifice. The kids get clothes and he gets clothes and I give myself nothing but what's left—and there is never much left. The only thing I don't hold back on is food. I eat it because I love it. I'm in control of how much I get, and no one can change that. When I diet, I take the one thing that I have away from myself. I deprive myself of my one source of pleasure. If I had it to do over again, I sure wouldn't do it as a doormat to anyone. And by the grace of God, my little girls aren't going to do it that way.

—A Fellow Struggler

PICTURES OF DEPRIVATION

Imagine a woman waking up from a nightmarish wreck on the high seas and finding herself on the white sand beach of a desert island. Fragments of the broken ship washed up on the shore. In a state of shock she looked around to see a few trees, some shrubs, and a small stream of water. There were no people on her island to help her survive. She was on her own. As the tremendous responsibility to survive sank in, she became overwhelmed at the task and wept until she fell asleep.

The next day she was awakened by the hot sun. She moved under the shade of a tree to protect herself as she plotted how to stay alive as long as she could in hopes of being rescued. She was no quitter. She was deprived of every convenience she had grown used to, but she found a way to gather enough food to keep her body alive. At times she almost went crazy from having no one to talk to, no one to share her fears and pain. Storms came and went, but her resolve to survive remained steadfast through every difficult moment.

Somehow she lived on that island for five years until she was rescued. At the start of her horrible experience, she was a healthy human being, both physically and emotionally. When they picked her up, she had excessive fears and anxieties. She feared boats of all sizes, people, and even food she once loved. Having been deprived of almost everything she needed to live an abundant life—things like relationships, a balanced diet, opportunities to help others, and goals far beyond just getting by from day to day—she needed nourishment and nurturing.

It was ironic that the deprived woman who had worked so hard to find a way to stay alive had such a hard time living after she was rescued. She continued to deprive herself of food she once enjoyed. Part of her eating problem was an emotional problem. She just could not forgive herself for being so stupid as to go on that ship at that time of the year. She tormented herself with a thousand "I should have known better's." She never reconnected with people. Finally, her unbalanced diet left her poor in health, and her lack of meaningful relationships left her poor in spirit. Within a couple of years she was dead.

COMPENSATING FOR DEPRIVATION

Imagine if you will another woman who was stranded on a desert island without anyone to care for her. She struggled like the first and somehow discovered a way to survive. Finally, she was rescued, and she made her way back to civilization. From the moment she set foot on dry land, it was as if she were determined to make up for the five years of deprivation she had spent on that island. As she tried to satisfy her appetites, her anger toward those who had convinced her to take the trip on the ship increased. She spent hours obsessing over all those people responsible for her disaster.

Unconsciously trying to medicate her deep pain, she ate everything in sight. Nothing could satisfy the hunger that burned within her for five long years. It wasn't just food she desired. She was also hungry for a sexual relationship. She sought it with little regard for anything other than passion, pleasure, and companionship.

She went through a series of one-night stands and demeaning relationships. Within two years she weighed 190 pounds. She wanted to share her body, but she felt that there were no more takers. In her pain, she saw no hope for ever having a fulfilling life. Finally, her two-year journey out of deprivation ended in despair when she took as many sleeping pills as were left in the bottle. She never woke up.

LOOKING FOR PAST DEPRIVATION

Since I asked you to imagine with me, you know that the stories are not true, but they have been played out in almost exact detail in the lives of thousands of people who have felt deprived at some point in their lives.

Maybe you were deprived of the essentials of life. You ate normally, but when it came to having your soul fed, you were malnourished. You needed unconditional love, but you got only standards you couldn't live up to. You needed someone to meet your needs, but you ended up meeting someone else's expectations.

The deprivation may have been even worse. You were robbed of all that you had left because you were abused. You were hurt by violence, emotional terrorism, or verbal torture. You feel that you have been living in a prisoner-of-war camp and you are the only captive.

Wherever your journey has been, most likely you understand the feeling of being deprived. You understand the feeling of a starving soul and a starving body that just can't get enough to satisfy. You know the futility of trying to find love and meaning in a world that could not find enough love to make up for its absence in your life. So as a deprived struggler, perhaps you turned to food in an attempt to medicate a wound that seemed to be beyond healing.

Once you understand the devastating effects of deprivation, you know that you cannot win by inflicting it upon yourself. You see how futile it is to expect positive long-term results from forcing yourself into periods of forced deprivation. When you do so, you lose your balance, and you lose your ability to make sound decisions about your future.

Once you truly understand deprivation, you no longer find it mysterious that people never win the weight-loss battle by depriving themselves of food they love. It may produce a temporary change in weight, but its long-term effects are devastating. Many people who walk the senseless path of deprivation gain back every ounce in a subconscious attempt to get back every ounce of pleasure that was missed from all the unconsumed calories. Of course, others become so skilled at depriving themselves of what they need that they never stop depriving themselves until they cease to exist, their spirits dry up, their hearts break, and the will to live is completely destroyed.

I hope that if you feel there is no hope, you will not succumb to that feeling. I hope that you will dig deep within yourself and reach far beyond yourself to ask God for strength to try a different way to find fulfillment. It is a way that does not include depriving yourself further. It is a way to make short steps toward long-term change that will bring new hope and meaning to your life. This plan is a gentle plan for people who have been treated too roughly by a very cruel world. It is for those who decide they have been deprived of enough and they will no longer inflict deprivation upon themselves.

A cruel world inflicts pain not only through acts of violence and emotional trauma but also through misinformation. You have been hurt and you have hurt yourself because you have listened to some lies of people more interested in profits than principles. They have told you life will be better if you find a way to do without the food you love and purchase the products they love to sell you. Whatever they are, they are tools of deprivation.

Choose fulfillment.

You need nourishment and nurturing. You need nutrition that will heal your body, and you need unconditional nurturing that will heal your soul. They are your only means by which to break the destructive cycle. You need to be fulfilled, and that fulfillment will come only when you decide to seek ways to find it for yourself. At all costs you must avoid the extremes: overindulging in food or bingeing on deprivation and self-punishment. Deprived people deprive others of what they need and deserve. Fulfilled people help others reach fulfillment.

I invite you to heal your deep wounds of emotional deprivation so you will no longer need to build a fortress of fat around your heart that seals everyone out of your life. Contrary to popular belief, misery does not love company. I invite you out of your isolated misery and back into a wonderful world where people really do love each other and care more about others than they do themselves. I invite you to decline a cruel world's invitation to abuse yourself with the false hopes of a quick fix and an instant solution. I invite you to begin a fulfilling journey by being gentle with yourself. So let's get started.

In the following chapters we will look at reducing your consumption of high-fat and high-sugar foods. Don't completely deprive yourself of all fat and sugar. That will only increase your sense of deprivation and lead to eventual relapse. Be gentle with yourself and ease into a new way of eating. Avoid the extremes and find satisfaction in the middle. That middle ground, that balance, allows your wounds to heal.

The Prayer of a Gentle Eater

Dear God, help me not repeat the pain of my past. Help me avoid the temptation to deprive myself. Help me find healing on solid, balanced middle ground. And when I find it, help me lead others there.

Chapter 8

Cutting the Fat
(But Not Completely)

I hate to admit it, but I am comforted by the fat I eat. In my hours of deepest isolation, when the world has shut me out and I the world, there is something satisfying about food filled with fat. I know it is killing me, but I love it. Find me a substitute for this silky and soft satisfier of my soul, and then perhaps I can lose some weight. But who will ever find a substitute for butter? Who will be able to make anything more luscious than whipped cream? How do people live without these staples? Who would want to anyway?

—A Fellow Struggler

HUNTING FOR TREASURE

If you are following this plan, gently changing your life for good, you are now ready to look at what you eat and figure out some ways that you could eat differently and continue to feel satisfied. Even at this important step, you are not ready to reduce the amount of food you eat. You just need to make some changes that will lead to less fat and calories consumed and less fat on the body. Not only is it possible to receive satisfaction with less fat, but it can become a very enjoyable new behavior associated with your eating habits. It can become a game in which you are always the winner.

The game I play is much like a treasure hunt. I am always hunting for a new product that can replace an old one that was too high in fat for me. The most common example is great-tasting frozen yogurt to replace high-fat ice cream. Some brands taste just as good as ice cream. Frozen yogurt has made my life much freer from guilt as well as reduced my fat intake.

Find ways to reduce fat intake.

Frozen yogurt is a relatively new product, but other traditional products can free you from some of the fat that may be keeping you overweight. When I moved to Laguna Beach, I discovered that it offered wonderful bakeries of all kinds. I regularly stopped by one to eat a bran muffin as it popped out of the oven. Since a bran muffin is healthy, I felt very good about the habit I was creating. The sad part was that it increased the size of my waist.

After talking to the owner of the little place that made the marvelous muffins, I learned that I had been eating about ten grams of fat, eight grams of sugar, and 350 calories. And that was all done in the name of making a healthy choice. I knew the habit had to go, but I didn't know what I could replace it with. Finally, I made the discovery of a lifetime that enabled me to continue to stop off at a place in the morning for a visit with the town folk and consume only 150 calories with no sugar and little fat. I found a place that made fresh bagels.

A NEW TRADITION

I became a bagel fanatic. That traditional food had all the ingredients of a modern-day health food. At first I missed the sweet taste of the muffins, but eventually, I craved the unsweet taste of bagels and the wonderful smell of the shop in which they were made. Now I buy them fresh at the bakery, bring them home, slice them, and freeze them so that I can enjoy one at any time.

Many other foods like bagels and yogurt can take the place of high-fat, high-calorie, and high-sugar foods. Many of them are listed in Section 2. Become an explorer whose life depends on finding the holy grail of fulfillment through nonfat or low-fat foods. You'll be surprised at how many of them there are and how satisfying they can be.

THE NATURAL DESIRE FOR FAT

If you begin to limit your intake of fat, you will have a tremendous urge to eat something high in fat occasionally. For example, I sometimes crave chocolate ice cream. Rather than beat yourself up over that urge, congratulate yourself for restricting your fat intake to the degree that your body has noticed and is demanding a correction. And if you choose to eat higher-fat foods periodically, the damage to the long-term results will be minimal.

Let's say you have decided to substitute nonfat yogurt at one hundred calories and ten fat grams per serving less than ice cream. If you make that substitution ten times in a month, you save yourself one thousand calories and one hundred fat grams. That change alone could result in a weight loss of over four pounds in one year. If once a month you splurge and eat ice cream to satisfy a craving for fat, you add only one-tenth more calories, and over the course of that year, you gain only an additional one-third pound or lose one-third pound less. The key is to space out the times when you feel compelled to satisfy the fat craving.

Once you enter into the game of substitution, finding new ways to satisfy old appetites with nonfat foods, you will lose weight. You will also feel more energy as your body is able to run on a more efficient fuel free from the fat sludge that clogs up the bloodstream. It is too bad that every six weeks, about 56,000 Americans die of heart disease, most of which is caused by a high-fat, high-calorie diet. Can you believe it? It doesn't have to be that way, and it doesn't have to be that painful to lower the fat consumption.

YOUR BODY, YOUR ENGINE

I don't know much about engines. It is a mystery to me how these things work off gasoline blowing up at the precisely timed explosion from a perfectly placed spark plug. However, I do know that some basic fundamentals about engines can apply to our bodies.

For bodies or engines to run, they must have fuel. We especially need fuel in times of change. If we are trying to redo old habits and integrate healthy ones into our routines, the worst thing we could do is to improperly fuel our engines. We need everything on our side if we are going to win.

The better the fuel, the more efficiently we will run. The worse the fuel, the worse we will run and feel. If we don't have enough quality fuel, we will feel the need to compensate for it by adding quantity. If the quantity of fuel we take in is more than the fuel we burn up, we increase our weight.

The point I am making is this: *if you want to crave less food, you must put a higher quality of food in your body.* You are not eating just because you are depressed or anxious. You are eating because your body wants to be nourished. The easiest way to improve the quality of your intake is to cut the fat and replace it with nutritious food you love to eat.

FOOLING OURSELVES ABOUT FAT

Often we find good food to eat, but we combine it with junky food, also. On one of my typical evenings out, I would hit the salad bar at a restaurant. I would fill my plate with extremely healthy ingredients and then pour tons of high-fat dressing on top. I also loved pasta and tuna and chicken salads, thick with mayonnaise. By the time I was finished, the percentage of calories from fat was the equivalent of a plate of french fries. It was a nice try, but the results were not there. I would top off the disastrous meal with a piece of hula pie full of ice cream on a shell of Oreo cookie crumbs. I justified it by the fact that everything I had eaten was from the salad bar. Who was I fooling? My best intentions usually wound up failing, and even when I thought I was eating a healthy diet, I was eating more and more fat and watching the weight go higher and higher.

Now I have no excuse to make that mistake again because I am aware of how much fat I take in from food. This fat reduction concept came together for me one day when I had what I call a brain flash. Flashing in my brain was this oft-quoted piece of wisdom: you are what you think about. I applied that concept to the body and realized that I must be what I eat. In other words, the percentage of fat on my body is most likely a very direct result of the percentage of fat in the food I am eating. If I felt like I was half fat, I was probably eating food that was about one-half fat. So I determined to find food that not only appeared low in fat because of the few number of fat grams it contained but also translated into a low percentage. I was amazed to find that many things I believed to be low in fat were not.

THE FAT FORMULA

An example is a piece of red meat. If I eat a four-ounce serving of beef with 400 calories and 20 grams of fat, it is probably a prime piece of beef but not what I would call quality fuel. To figure how many of these calories are from fat, I can do a simple calculation. Each gram of fat has 9 calories. By multiplying 20 (the number of fat grams in the meat) times 9, I come up with 180. I now know that 180 of the total calories are from fat, and since the total calories are 400, I create the ratio of 180 to 400, fat calories to total calories. Dividing 400 into 180 gives me a final percentage of fat calories: 45 percent.

If all I ever ate was that type of meat, 45 percent of my calories would come from fat. That is too much. And often people have no idea of the percentage of calories from fat. Even products advertising 95 percent fat-free can have a very high percentage of fat in each serving. Nutritionists measure fat content in terms of calories. Advertisers prefer to measure fat content in terms of weight because that sounds better. So a product praised as 95 percent fat-free (by *weight*) may actually contain 30 percent to 40 percent fat by *calories*. Be on the lookout for foods that may be putting fat on you while you think you are eating wisely.

The formula can reassure you that you are on the right track with the right low-fat food. Consider a can of vegetable soup. Each serving has 90 calories and 2 grams of fat ($2 \times 9 = 18$ and $18 \div 90 = 20\%$), so 20 percent of the calories come from fat. A food with 20 percent fat would be better for you than one with 45 percent fat. You really do become what you eat. If you make a change and begin to eat lean, you are going to look more and more lean as you move closer to your weight-loss goal.

If I can do it, you can do it. Just make the decision to get started with the priority of being gentle with yourself through your loss of weight.

Remember that the formula for determining the percentage of fat is as follows: the number of fat grams multiplied by nine calories per gram divided by the total number of calories in the food. The more you do the equation, the easier it becomes. You can become quite an expert at monitoring the number of fat grams you are eating and the percentage of calories coming from fat. When you gently lower both figures, you watch your figure transform.

Step 6: Replace high-fat foods with foods that are lower in fat.

If you set a goal of eating an average of 10 percent or even 20 percent of your calories from fat, you will succeed in calorie reduction and weight loss. Figures 8.1 and 8.2 show how many grams of fat you could consume, depending on sex, weight, and average calories per day. Before you start limiting your fat intake, consult your physician to get individual guidance specifically suited for your body and your health condition.

Goal of Calories from Fat		10%	20%
Weight	Calories	Fat Grams	Fat Grams
130	2200	24	49
140	2400	27	53
150	2600	29	58
160	2700	30	60
170	2900	32	64
180	3100	34	69
190	3200	36	71
200	3400	38	76
210	3600	40	80
220	3700	41	82

FIGURE 8.1. Fat goals for men participating
in regular exercise

(From *Prevention* magazine, July 1992, p. 40.)

Goal of Calories from Fat		10%	20%
Weight	Calories	Fat Grams	Fat Grams
100	1500	17	33
110	1700	19	38
120	1800	20	40
130	2000	22	44
140	2100	23	47
150	2300	26	51
160	2400	27	53
170	2600	29	58

**FIGURE 8.2. Fat goals for women participating
in regular exercise**

(From *Prevention* magazine, July 1992, p. 40.)

LOW-FAT SUBSTITUTIONS

After you determine your goal, you will want to find new ways to achieve it without depriving yourself of all the things you like. You can make the following substitutions to lower the fat intake in your diet. The more you are able to substitute and find satisfaction in the substitute, the more likely your plan will lead to long-term results.

High-Fat Food	Low-Fat Substitute
Potato chips	Pretzels
	Baked tortilla chips
	Crunchy vegetables
Cheese sauce	Grated nonfat cheese
	Tomato sauce
	Chopped garlic
Popcorn popped in oil	Hot air-blown popcorn
	Low-fat microwave popcorn

High-Fat Food	Low-Fat Substitute
Popcorn popped in oil *(cont'd)*	Nonfat butter sprinkle product
	Low-fat grated cheese rather than butter
Fried fish	Baked fish
	Broiled fish
	Steamed fish
Chocolate chip cookies	Nonfat cookies
	Nonfat brownies
	Vanilla wafers
	Graham crackers
	Fig bars
Salmon	Flounder
	Cod
	Bass
Doughnuts	Bagels
	Low-fat cake
	Nonfat muffins
Crackers	Melba toast
	Bagel chips
Oil-packed tuna	Freshwater-packed tuna
Croissant	Bagel
	Sourdough roll
Granola	Nonfat granola
	Round oat cereal
	Any nonfat, low-sugar cereal
Cheddar cheese	Nonfat Swiss
	Part skim mozzarella
Cream cheese	Nonfat cream cheese
	Farmer cheese
Sour cream	Nonfat yogurt

High-Fat Food	Low-Fat Substitute
Butter	Nonstick cooking spray
	Trace of olive oil
	Fruit spread (e.g., apple butter)
Mayonnaise	Mustard
	Low-fat spread
	Yogurt
Processed sandwich meats (e.g., salami and bologna)	Sliced turkey or chicken
Ground beef	Ground turkey
	Ground chicken
	Vegetable patty
Bacon	Imitation bacon bits
	Turkey sausage

GOOD FAT, BAD FAT

The more fat you consume that comes from plants rather than animals, the better it will be for you. (There are only a few exceptions such as palm oil and coconut oil.) If you can gradually shift from one kind to the other, you are going to do yourself and your heart a favor.

The bad kind of fat is saturated fat, and it comes in the forms of butter, meat, and lard—all products of animals. You see these types of fats most often in solid form if they are at room temperature. The good fat, unsaturated fat, is liquid at room temperature; there are polyunsaturated and mono-unsaturated fats. (The terms *good* and *bad* are not in reference to the amount of fat or calories; they are in reference to the damage done to the heart when consumed in mass quantities.)

Polyunsaturated fats are found in oils like corn, sunflower, safflower, soybean, and sesame. Olive oil and canola oil are monounsaturated fats, and they tend to be better for you than all the rest. Using monounsaturated fats can lower your levels of low-density lipoprotein, or LDL, which is the bad kind of cholesterol. High-density lipoprotein, or HDL, is a good kind of cholesterol that helps you fight heart disease.

A good guide, if you are able to track the type of fat you consume, works like this. You should limit your total calorie intake from fat to less than one-third. Less than one-third of that total fat should come from polyunsaturated fat. Less than one-third of the fat should come from saturated fat sources. A little more than one-third of the fat should come from monounsaturated sources. Stick to this guide, and you will have a balanced diet that is satisfying yet fat-portion proper.

REMEMBERING THE GENTLE APPROACH

Again, we must go back to the central theme of the book: the changes you make in every area must be very gentle. You must gradually alter what you are doing and get used to it before you go on to the next step. Becoming a crusader against fat is not an instant process, and if one day you begin eating foods that contain no fat at all, you will fail on your plan while doing something unbalanced and unhealthy. Your body needs some fat to function. You don't want to deprive it, or it will turn on you, overtake your best intentions, and destroy the progress you make. So gently change the fat content of your diet, and break the rules every now and then to ensure you can endure over the long haul of your new eating plan.

The Prayer of a Gentle Eater

Dear God, help me change what I eat from something that hurts me to something that helps me. Help me stop long enough to make some small decisions that will change life in a large way. Thank You for giving me the courage to change some old habits that have been with me a long time. Thank You for hope.

Chapter 9

Sugar

Sugar makes me emotionally ill. It gives me a high, and then it throws me into the dark dungeon of depression. There is no value in knowing this because I repeat it over and over again. Sugar plus me equals guilt. But I do love it so. And it seems so healthy, coming out of the ground from beets and cane. There's just nothing like it. I wish it didn't have so many side effects. Shouldn't the surgeon general label it with a warning that it can ruin your life? Oh, well, the warning would probably just entice me to do it even more. Before sugar, life must have been horrible.

—A Fellow Struggler

THE UNIQUE EFFECTS OF SUGAR

The sugar blues are a reality for only a segment of the population, but they are a reality for more people than realize it. Many people seek help, and they are so emotionally distraught that they say they will do anything to change. They will do anything but look at some of their behaviors that may be leading to their negative feelings.

One overweight woman experienced the highs and lows of manic-depression. When she was up, she was way up, and she felt good. But when she landed, it was always a crash landing. She was so sad that she cried at the slightest upset. As her period approached, she grew irritable and anxious, and she satisfied her edginess with a lot of chocolate saturated with sugar. The edginess passed with her period, but a deepening depression remained. She just thought she had a severe PMS cycle that she would have to live with.

Insight from a nutritionist led to change, and that change led to a lighter body and a freer mind. She weaned herself off chocolate in the days before her period. Rather than eat something high in calories, high in fat, and low in nutrition, she convinced herself that at those times of the month, she should be eating things to give her body a nutritious lift. She became a connoisseur of fruits. On the days before her period, she upped her fruit intake; she ate fruits served in every way imaginable. She replaced a piece of flavored, sugary fat with a nutritious piece of fruit. The results were astounding.

She was being gentle with herself. She was caring for herself, and that made her feel great about herself. What a change to go from making the problem worse to fighting the problem! Her moods stabilized, her periods were less troublesome, and she began to lose weight. When her period stopped, the depression she previously experienced did not take its place.

Keep an hourly eating record.

That kind of breakthrough can happen to you. It takes a little effort to analyze the patterns of your moods and correlate them with your diet, but if you do, you may discover some ways to change a habit or two that will alter the way you feel and think about yourself.

CHARTING THE EFFECTS OF FOOD

Here is a format that can help you. It requires paper, pencil, and an alarm clock. My watch has an alarm, and that works best for me because it is portable. I tend to get up around 5:00 A.M. so that's when my chart starts. Every hour I list the food that I eat and the mood that I am in. I set my alarm on my watch to go off every hour so I won't forget. I record my feelings from 1 to 10 (1 being the worst I could feel and 10 being the best).

Time	Food	Feelings
5:00 A.M.	Hot decaf tea	5
6:00 A.M.	Apple	
	Bagel	6
7:00 A.M.	Hot tea	7
8:00 A.M.	Nothing	7
9:00 A.M.	Nothing	7
10:00 A.M.	Hot tea	
	Bagel	8
11:00 A.M.	Water	7
12:00 Noon	Vegetable soup	
	White rice	
	Frozen yogurt	
	Iced tea	7
1:00 P.M.	Nothing	8
2:00 P.M.	Nothing	6
3:00 P.M.	Water	5

Time	Food	Feelings
4:00 P.M.	Water	5
5:00 P.M.	Nothing	4
6:00 P.M.	Pasta	
	Salad	
	Corn	
	Apple pie	7
7:00 P.M.	Nothing	7
8:00 P.M.	Popcorn	6
9:00 P.M.	Nothing	
10:00 P.M.	Sleep	
11:00 P.M.	Sleep	
12:00 Midnight	Sleep	
1:00 A.M.	Sleep	
2:00 A.M.	Sleep	
3:00 A.M.	Sleep	
4:00 A.M.	Sleep	

You have no idea how I wish I ate like that every day. But it just isn't so. This chart gives me some insight into myself even when I am eating great. First of all, it shows that I am a morning person. I really do feel much better from

Analyze your food diary for insight.

6:00 A.M. until about 2:00 P.M. than I do any other time of day. It also shows that if I would eat a piece of fruit in the afternoon, I would probably be in a little better mood when I arrived home. But forget about me. Let's look at a typical overeater's chart in the midst of some very heavy eating and how that might affect feelings.

Time	Food	Feelings
5:00 A.M.	Sleep	
6:00 A.M.	Coffee	
	Cream	
	Sugar	
	Sweet roll	
	Bacon	
	Eggs	
	Potatoes	
	Orange juice	7
7:00 A.M.	Doughnut	6
8:00 A.M.	Coffee	
	Cream	
	Sugar	
	Muffin	5
9:00 A.M.	Coffee	
	Cream	
	Sugar	
	Doughnut	5
10:00 A.M.	Coffee	
	Cream	
	Sugar	
	Chocolate bar	4
11:00 A.M.	Water	4
12:00 Noon	Cheeseburger	
	Fries	
	Cola	
	Chocolate sundae	5
1:00 P.M.	Nothing	4
2:00 P.M.	Cola	4

Time	Food	Feelings
3:00 P.M.	Cola	3
4:00 P.M.	Water	3
5:00 P.M.	Nothing	2
6:00 P.M.	Fried chicken	
	Mashed potatoes	
	Gravy	
	Corn	
	Rolls	
	Apple pie	
	Chocolate cake	3
7:00 P.M.	Nothing	3
8:00 P.M.	Ice cream	2
9:00 P.M.	Cookies and milk	2
10:00 P.M.	Sleep	
11:00 P.M.	Sleep	
12:00 Midnight	Sleep	
1:00 A.M.	Sleep	
2:00 A.M.	Sleep	
3:00 A.M.	Sleep	
4:00 A.M.	Sleep	

FINDING THE PATTERN

If that were the actual pattern of someone who wanted my advice, I would conclude that as he eats more and more, he feels worse and worse, except for a couple of times during the day. He may not be a morning person, but his eating habits make the morning the best time of day for him.

Another pattern might be a roller-coaster effect throughout the day that went up and down rather than consistently down. That pattern would be reflected in a person who was much more sensitive to the rise and fall of her blood sugar level and felt it emotionally when it went up and down.

The goal of any program should be to help you maintain very consistent mood levels so you are not tempted to go out of control when you soar to the heights on sugar (and caffeine) or when you plummet into depression as the sugar level drops.

Tomorrow begin to chart yourself, and see what you discover. *Don't* cheat yourself by neglecting to record what you eat as precisely as possible. Be honest with yourself about how you really feel. You're doing this for your benefit. You may want to keep it up for at least a week to get an accurate picture.

AVOIDING HIGH SUGAR CONTENT

The hidden sugar processed into some foods is detrimental to a healthy eating plan. Breakfast cereal is a particularly guilty culprit. When you buy breakfast cereal, you need to look at the fat content and the sugar per serving. The serving will probably be one-half to one-third the amount you normally pour into your bowl.

One cereal I was looking at the other day contained fifteen grams of sugar per serving. The serving size was so small that I definitely would have had three servings to fill my bowl. A teaspoon of sugar contains about four grams. That means at three servings of fifteen grams of sugar each, I would have consumed forty-five grams of sugar—or over eleven teaspoons of sugar—from one bowl of cereal.

Even the greatest sugar lovers in the world would have a hard time dumping eleven teaspoons of sugar on their cereal, but if they eat some brands in any quantity, that is exactly what they are doing. Is it any wonder they will have to continue to eat sugary foods all day just to keep going?

The blood sugar level will skyrocket and then plummet so low they will have to fight to get it back to normal.

A little knowledge can prevent you from having your efforts at weight loss sabotaged by the food industry. And what applies to cereal applies to some of the new nonfat foods. Manufacturers cut the fat and add so much sugar that you will gain just as much weight because the body will take all the excess sugar calories and turn them into fat.

If you become an alert buyer, you can continue to use sugar moderately and greatly reduce the amount you get from processed food. You will not even feel that you are giving anything up, and yet switching two or three products could save you as much as three hundred calories a day. If you could do that and continue to use table sugar, you wouldn't need to use artificial sweeteners that don't taste very good, don't satisfy, and produce little change in the people using them.

Step 7: Lower your intake of foods that are high in sugar.

I drank a lot of diet drinks until I realized that only overweight people drink them—well, that is almost the case. But I don't see many people walking around twenty pounds lighter than they were last year because of their consumption of diet drinks. I wonder if the long-term effect of sugar substitutes might be an increase in sodium, an increase in a potentially carcinogenic substance, and an increase in calories due to some fluke of metabolism. If sugar substitutes work for you, fine. They don't for me, and I don't use them. I just watch the processed foods and cut out large sugar quantities.

Your biggest problem in losing weight and keeping it off is not sugar. Your biggest problem is fat. You should spend twice as much time concentrating on eating less fat than you do on eating less sugar. But you cannot go out of control on sugar consumption and expect to lose weight. Too much sugar will be converted to fat. A gentle approach is to watch your sugar intake and try to lower it gradually. Read the labels and make healthy choices for yourself.

The Prayer of a Gentle Eater

Dear God, help me make another step toward looking and feeling my best. Help me delay some of my desire. Please help me reach the victory I want so I can savor the sweetness of success. I want to like myself better.

Chapter 10

Eating More to Weigh Less— The Multiple Meal Concept

I can't believe how well I do during the day only to completely fail in the evening. I skip breakfast, and I can make it all the way to lunch without one calorie getting into my body. I don't feel tired or worn out. I feel fine. At lunch I eat very little. I'm satisfied with a salad or a bowl of soup. Then I sit down to dinner, and I reward myself for all the food I passed up in the day. I can't stop eating until I go to bed. Some nights I go to bed at eight o'clock just to stop eating, but I usually get back up because I get hungry. And who can go to sleep at eight, anyway? At night I leave no food group untapped. I cover it all, and it still is not enough. You know, it's strange. It seems that the only food I don't have room for is Jell-O. Now why is that?

—A Fellow Struggler

METABOLISM

The universal plight of overweight dieters is too much effort to obtain too few results. Some of the most hard-core programs are self-inflicted by those who are using all their might to lose weight. They create rigid schedules and guidelines. They make up rules to prove they are in control, such as no food until noon. Yet these restrictions have the opposite effect from what these people want.

When the day starts with no food after a night of no food, the body sounds an alarm. The body believes that since no food is put into it, there is no food available. It goes into starvation mode, preparing to live off as few calories as possible. The metabolism slows so that the available calories will be used gradually.

Through the ages, the body has grown accustomed to going hungry in the winter rather than the summer. When no food is available, the body thinks it's winter even if it's 120 degrees in the shade. The body slows down the calorie burn and stores fat whenever possible. Many of us normally pick up five pounds each winter because of this reaction of the body to cold. Others of us gain five pounds every season, no matter what the temperature, because we unknowingly give the body the message that a cold winter is upon us and there is not much food.

If you eat only between noon and midnight, your body may stand on hunger alert for the other half of the day. Your slowed metabolism creates more fat from food than with those who are on hunger alert only six to eight hours a day. The good news is, there is a way to solve it that leaves you with less fat, more food, and more satisfaction. When you start being good to yourself, stop starving and depriving, and start gently meeting your needs, you lose more weight and keep it off for good.

GAINING AND MAINTAINING CONTROL

The key to this metabolism change and the ability to stay in control of your food intake is obvious from the title of the chapter. You need to start rewarding yourself with more meals. That doesn't mean you will eat twice as many calories or twice as much fat, but that does mean you will gain control of your hunger rather than let it run away with you while your body is slowly metabolizing whatever you consume into fat. You will gain that control with six small meals rather than three or two big meals.

Step 8: Eat more meals a day while taking in the same number of calories.

You may be thinking that this way of eating will not work for you. You know that once you take a bite of anything, you are out of control for the rest of the day. You hold off until noon because you know you have avoided about a thousand calories from just waiting. You have seen it happen too many times that when you get asked out to breakfast, it is a lost day because you will eat all morning long. Your feelings are valid, but the results are not what you think.

You must convince yourself that even if you avoid the one thousand calories, the other three thousand or four thousand you get will enter a slowed metabolism geared to make fat. Your only hope is to break the cycle and allow yourself to feel more satisfaction over time. The following schedule is a great way for you to stay in control of your hunger so your hunger doesn't take control of you:

8:00 A.M.	Piece of fruit
	Toasted bagel
10:00 A.M.	Piece of fruit
	Toasted bagel
12:00 Noon	Turkey sandwich
	Carrot sticks
	One piece of nonfat cake
2:30 P.M.	Bowl of soup
	Crackers
	Low-fat cheese
	Nonfat milk
5:30 P.M.	Pasta
	Tomato sauce
	French bread
	Grilled vegetables
	Low-sugar fruit cobbler
7:30 P.M.	Frozen yogurt
	Fruit

MAINTAINING
THE SCHEDULE

If you took each entry on that schedule and substituted something else of like value on a different day, you would have an effective diet plan with enough protein, fat, and carbohydrates to nourish you while avoiding high-sugar and high-fat foods. This schedule wouldn't just help you win from a metabolic and physiological standpoint; it would also help you win emotionally. You would feel in control of your emotions and your eating habits.

A dilemma regarding eating more meals comes when you are on the run or in a car for most of your day. Can you think of a time when you saw someone in a car eating something healthy? Usually, it's a burrito or a hamburger.

One solution is to plan ahead. Buy a small cooler to keep in the car. Load it up with low-calorie and low-fat foods, such as carrot sticks, fruits, cut vegetables, nonfat cheese, nonfat yogurt, and fruit drinks. If you know you'll have a few minutes, pull over at a scenic spot on your route, and have a salad prepared with nonfat dressing. Another idea would be a pasta salad with herbs, spices, and nonfat Italian dressing. Several varieties of meals suggested in Section 2 can be stored until lunch in your cooler.

When I pack food for a busy day on the road, I throw in a bagel or two, a banana, fresh carrot juice, and anything else that is low in fat and easy to manage even while driving. This idea will help you gain independence and maintain control of your food and your life. And if you ever get trapped in a snowstorm, you will survive with your little cooler full of healthy food.

By planning ahead and packing your lunch or snack foods, you will be sure to have a healthy, satisfying lunch or snack, and you will be amazed at how much money you will save over a period of time. You will need that money to purchase a new wardrobe or to alter the clothes you now have because they will be too big for you one day.

FAST FOOD

If you have to eat on the run, sooner or later you are going to be forced to run into a fast-food place. It is better to eat in a fast-food place and stick to your schedule than it is to skip a meal and alarm your metabolism to slow down for winter. Don't despair. These establishments have come a long way in accommodating the healthy eater. In many you can order a baked potato with a side salad. Then use your own dressing that contains no fat and low sodium. Many fast-food restaurants charbroil their food, so you might order a skinless chicken breast with a salad and/or baked potato. Again use your own dressing with no fat and low sodium.

Many fast-food restaurants offer full salad bars. Remember to avoid the cheese, pasta items, and other items (e.g., eggs, bacon bits, diced meat) that will turn your low-fat, low-calorie salad into a high-fat, high-calorie meal. Be creative in your selection so that you don't get bored.

THE HUNGER MONSTER

If you struggle like I do, you struggle with an imaginary being inside called the hunger monster. The hunger monster is fine to live with as long as it is fed regularly.

Food makes the monster small, and anger makes the monster large. The longer it goes without food, the angrier and bigger the monster gets. It can become so big that you can no longer control it. You end up at its mercy, and it carries you off to the kitchen and forces you to eat even when you don't really want to. It is angry, and it will punish you by making you do things you don't want to do and eat things you don't want to eat. The hunger monster is a master at shaming you and attacking your self-esteem.

My advice to you: don't mess with the hunger monster. Meet its needs on a regular basis. Keep it small so that you are always more powerful than it is. If you don't, you are going to have a tough time shrinking that monster. Respect the hunger monster and you will always have it working with you rather than destroying your efforts to control your weight. Keep the monster satisfied with more small meals consumed on schedule.

PORTION CONTROL

Once you gain control of your schedule, you can gradually expand that level of control to the portions you choose to eat. If you choose reasonable portions of the foods that satisfy you the most, you will be less likely to binge to overcome a sense of deprivation. Diets from the past have taught you that to lose weight, you must be deprived. If you struggle with compulsive overeating, you know by now that system always leads to a binge. Or you take the weight off only to put it back on again—with a few additional pounds. Planning ahead with your meals can prevent bingeing.

Eat reasonable portions.

As you eat healthy low-fat and low-calorie foods, you need to find your safety zone of the portions. The more you control the portions, the greater your rewards will be. It takes a little effort and some thought. After you eat a meal, ask yourself how you feel. Are you satisfied? Are you still hungry or feeling stuffed? Answering these questions will help you gauge your future meals as far as the portions that satisfy you without overdoing it.

Your goal is to find out how much food you need to feel satisfied and eat that much. You must learn to use food as a source to nourish yourself and eat when you experience true hunger. Then when you eat six or seven times a day, you'll get reasonable amounts of food, full of nutrients but lacking much of the fat you are used to. When you break old deprivation patterns, control is your gift to yourself.

The Prayer of a Gentle Eater

Dear God, help me gain control of my eating habits. I so want to feel good at the end of the day. Let me control my appetite. I am willing to try a new way. Give me the strength to persevere.

Chapter 11

Relationships with Things Other Than Food

Last night it happened again. He made me look like a fool in front of his friends. So what if I thought Africa was a country? He didn't have to laugh out loud and call me Dumbo. He does it to the kids, too. Anything he knows that they don't or anytime they trip or fall, he uses it to make himself look like a superior human. I hate it. So I eat. I eat at him, not with him. I know I deserve better. I know it could be different and things could change. I just don't know how to get there from here.

—A Fellow Struggler

HELPFUL AND HURTFUL RELATIONSHIPS

You need a wide variety of gentle relationships. But most of your relationships may be overly demanding. If you can change the nature of your hurtful relationships, you can win your weight-loss battles with much less effort because you will have an army around you helping you. Let's examine some relationships that may be hurting you but could turn into relationships that help you.

A RELATIONSHIP WITH THE CREATOR

First, let's look at the God who created you. Let's consider how a relationship with God the Creator, your Creator, may be hurting you but could be helping you. I always find it fascinating how a person's view of God can affect every other area of life—especially someone who claims not to have a relationship with God. Trust me. You have a relationship with God. The only question is whether or not you acknowledge it.

Step 9: Work on relationships with things other than food.

Few people are actually convinced there is no God. In view of all the new archeological and scientific discoveries, many so-called avowed atheists are finding their position to be very weak. One scientist was able to capture what the creation of the universe might have been like through microwave technology. He said it was like looking into the face of God. The discoveries of ancient biblical cities such as Sodom and Gomorrah, cities that many thought were part of ancient myths, now further point to the historical accuracy of the Bible. If you have never taken the time to read some stories from the Old Testament, I think you will be intrigued by them and the central theme running through them that can be of great inspiration.

That theme is this: people are faithful to God until there is a famine or a tough time of some sort. Then the people fall away from God or grow weak in their faith. God's love reaches out to them, and the relationship is restored—or you could say the people find peace with God once again.

God hasn't changed, and neither have we. We are still going through those same cycles and patterns. That is why I believe everyone has a relationship with God. It's just that we are at various stages in the relationship. Are we at the initial faithful stage? Are we at the tough part? Have we turned away? Or are we on the way back to restoring a relationship with God?

Understanding the World as It Is

I have met many people who are feeding old wounds from childhood that they relate to God. For instance, they blame God for the death of a parent or the divorce of their parents. They think that the terrible thing happened because God didn't care about them or He caused it. These folks feel this way because they have unrealistic expectations of God.

Imagine a world where God protected everyone from everything. Everyone who got sick got healed. Every time a car crash was about to happen, a big rubber ball was dropped from heaven between the two vehicles, and they bounced safely off each other. In a world like that, you couldn't make a mistake because there would be no consequences to any action. If you grew angry and wanted to hit someone, an air bag would fly out of the other guy's face and protect him from the blow. You could jump off a building and land safely because your suicide would hurt others so you would live to protect them.

What I just described would be heaven to live in, but this isn't heaven. In our world, we make mistakes and pay the consequences. In our world, others make mistakes, and we suffer the consequences. If we drive drunk and crash, we can get killed or maimed. If someone else drives drunk and crashes into us, we can get killed or maimed.

It isn't fair, but one of the first signs of maturity is realizing the world is not fair and does not revolve around you. In our world, big fish eat little fish, and dishonest people often get more than honest people. It is so unfair that if you try to live it on your own, without the help of God, the chances are about ten out of ten that you will fail.

What a relief to understand that God is not a bellhop in the sky waiting to wait on us! And we overeaters like nothing more than to have someone wait on us. Although God does not protect us from all the potential evil in the world and does not prevent us from making some spectacular mistakes with our lives, He will use all the good, the bad, and the ugly for our good. Some of the worst things that happen to us dredge out the very depths of our character, give us endurance and strength, and often send us off on a new life mission.

I feel sorry for people who are so caught up in wondering why God didn't spare them some tragedy that they refuse to get on with their lives. I can only hope and pray that one day their "why me?" will turn into a mature "why *not* me?" I pray that the focus of those who are wasting their lives avoiding God would finally turn to how they could take their hurts and use them to serve God better.

God is big enough to have a plan for each individual. We need to find out God's plan for us and discover what we can do to serve God rather than demand that He serve us.

A New View of the Pew

You may not have developed your relationship with God because of a traumatic experience with a church. You may have been spiritually abused or constantly shamed. You may have been led to feel that you didn't belong. You may have left the church, believing that God doesn't really love you. These unfortunate things happen when small people become responsible for large numbers of people.

I encourage you not to judge all churches based on your experience. Many churches work hard to be places where people are served and needs are met. Many churches have opened new doors through support groups and counseling programs. They are places to heal. If the church is the first place people call when someone dies, it should also be the first place people call when someone decides to live. For it is in living that we need God to help us and encourage us and motivate us to continue, even in the tough times.

Finding the Gentleness of God

Some people would love to turn to God, but they are afraid. They feel that God is an angry force who wants to do nothing more than spoil the party. First of all, what is going on in most people's lives is far from a party. They are miserable, and they fake it by appearing to have a great time. Second, although God is a just God, God is also a very loving God.

Discover God's gentleness.

My picture of God comes straight out of the New Testament. When God sent His Son, Jesus, to earth, He said that if you have seen the Son, you have seen the Father. In other words, the life of Jesus reveals certain things that are true about the character and nature of God.

My favorite portrait of God was detailed on the day when

Jesus was very busy and His followers were concerned that all the important people see Him. They tried to remove the little children from Him so He would not be bothered by them. Jesus would have none of that, and He told His followers to allow the children to come to Him. My picture of Jesus replaces one of those children with me, and I draw close to Him and He accepts me just the way I am today. He is, more than anything, gentle with me. That picture motivates me to live for Him rather than run from Him.

A ship without a rudder, a boat without a sail—both will have major problems going where the sailor wants to go. There may be a lot of flurry and activity, but if there isn't a rudder or a sail, all the effort in the world will not enable a vessel to sail on course. You may have set out on your journey without a sail or a rudder. You may be the ultimate crusader for self-help. I invite you to consider what it would be like to allow God to help you. God helps people every day. You can become one of them once you humble yourself enough to realize that your problems are much too big for you to manage and conquer alone.

I love the old story of the sailor who had instructions to outfit the ship and set sail in record time. He did his job, and as he was sailing out past the harbor entrance, word came from the captain. The sailor knew it would be some mention of the fine job he had done. When the sailor heard the message being read, he realized it had been radioed to the ship: "Nice job, but one of the first rules of the open sea is to never set sail until you are sure the captain is on board."

If you failed many times at changing your life by changing your weight, I wonder if you failed because you embarked on your journey without a captain on board. Ask God to guide your actions and be with you in the tough times. Admit that you can't do it on your own, and then allow Him to help. That could be a life-changing prayer for you as it has been for thousands of people with problems similar to yours.

Relationships are important to a plan to change your life. So many people try to put all their earthly relationships together but never stop to think about their relationship with God. I believe that these people run on empty: their lives are empty, and they wonder if there could possibly be more to life. They try every new philosophy, which only prevents them from becoming all they can become in a relationship with the God who created them. I invite you to begin the most incredible journey of your life, the journey toward a relationship with the true and wonderful and powerful and loving God of the universe.

THE RELATIONSHIPS AROUND YOU

Once you have started to work on your relationship with God, you're ready to work on your relationships with other people. In this regard, your most significant and defining relationship is the one with your parents. What they etch on your soul is hard to erase. Those of us who overeat often have some very strange etchings, such as the pattern of overindulgence.

Quite frankly, your parents may have spoiled you. They may have protected you from some of the pain in life and given you everything you wanted. As you grew up and felt the normal struggles we all experience, you may have repeated the overindulgence in the area of food, drink, credit spending, and a whole assortment of activities taken to an unhealthy extreme. To get to maturity, you must realize that life is tough but manageable. You can endure and enjoy it.

At the other extreme are parents who abuse physically, emotionally, sexually, and even spiritually. You may have come from a home where one or both parents could be described as evil. You may have wasted much of your life in your attempts to get back at them or get even. Although it could be a lifelong journey, you somehow need to get on the path toward forgiving your parents. You will have to pass through points of denial, anger, rage, blame, shame, and disregard. But if you persevere, at the end of the road you will be able to forgive them and thus free yourself from their grasp.

Replicating the Past

When you do not forgive, you often set out not to be like your parents. Everything you do is in reaction to them. The sad result is, you end up acting just like them. Let me explain it this way. Let's say that a great parent is a 10, your parents were 3s, and you have the potential to be an 8. You want to be an 8, but it's hard because you were raised by 3s. You determine not to make the mistakes of 3-grade parents. You focus on what your 3s did to you so that you will be sure not to repeat the mistakes. You become so focused on 3 behavior and doing better that you land just above a 3—perhaps at 3.5. If you want to be a transitional generation and change your outcome, you have to focus on what 10s would do rather than 3s.

I know that is an oversimplification, but it explains to a degree how victims become victimizers, how unresolved wounds from our parents are reproduced in our children. Some of us are overweight, and we are producing overweight children because we are trapped in old unresolved issues with our parents. When we let go of those old issues, we somehow loosen the grip our parents have on us. Our behavior becomes our own rather than a reaction to others' mistakes.

The Choices of Love

If you are single, the people you date have a lot to do with how well you achieve your goal of a complete and lasting change. Perhaps you date someone who loves to go to a Mexican restaurant for multiple baskets full of fried tortilla chips and other fried fare. After a night out, the person leads you back to the house for a late night television marathon topped off with some ice cream and cake. You may feel satisfied that you are with someone, but that someone may be preventing you from becoming who you want to become. Few of us could resist the temptation to consume high-calorie foods if confronted by them night after night.

Or perhaps you date someone with a different idea of how to spend time together. The person prefers an evening of working out together—side by side on exercycles or treadmills. You play volleyball or tennis on weekends. The dating relationship is characterized by doing healthy things like taking walks and having picnics with healthy food.

One quick note on a major issue for singles—the problem of abusive relationships. When you are single, you see dating partners at their best, and although you might think marriage would change someone, it does not. It only intensifies poor behavior. If I could instill one thought into the minds of insecure people, it would be this: being without a relationship is better than being in an abusive one. Millions of people would rather put up with anything than be alone. If you are not used to someone treating you gently, you will settle for someone treating you any way that person chooses. I encourage you to rethink your actions. Believe that it would be better for you to be gentle with yourself alone than have a relationship with someone who will abuse you.

Ask your companion to encourage you.

If you are struggling with your weight and you are in a dating relationship, your best hope is to tell that person what you are struggling with and request help. Ask for encouragement. If that person sabotages your good efforts, recognize that marriage or any relationship with that person would probably not work out. There would always be a need for superiority that prevented you from becoming what you want to become. Walk away now, and you may be able to walk into the future you want.

The Uncomfortable Marriage

If you are married, I don't need to tell you how difficult it is to lose weight if the other person is not cooperative. Many marriages are one marriage counselor away from being stabilized. People struggle and refuse to get help, but if they would just humble themselves to get it, they would find that many of their problems have a fairly simple solution.

Perhaps you are in a marriage that seems hopelessly uncomfortable. Your partner abuses you or refuses to be faithful. You are driven to comforting yourself with food.

I know those relationships exist, but even they have some hope. I urge you not to give up on the relationship until you have tried to get the other person into counseling, you've gotten counseling for yourself, and both of you have been counseled together. The problems of the other person may be so severe that treatment is required. You may need treatment. Get it sooner than later. So often those who divorce discover they have replaced one problem for a different set of problems. Don't let that happen to you. Work and pray and believe that your marriage can work for you until you have exhausted every resource and alternative.

I could never address all the complexities of the marriage relationship. Each person deserves a gentle marriage characterized by comfort and peace, encouragement and support. If you don't have that, your efforts to change will be tougher but not impossible. In fact, your progress may motivate your spouse to work on personal problems. Taking the focus off the other person often frees the other person to get busy.

Work on yourself to become the best you can become, and see if that produces a positive change in your spouse. *If* your change has no effect or makes matters worse, you can at least feel you have done everything possible to help the marriage. But until you have gone to work on yourself, you cannot expect the other person to wake up one day and decide to start treating you differently.

Kids and the Control Factor

After the marriage relationship comes the issue of children. The frustration of being a parent, especially a single one, can cause you to overeat as a means of comfort. If your children are driving you to eat, think about the area of control. Who is in control at your house? You or the children? If they are in control, it is time you took back control.

Perhaps your children have become the entire focus of your life. This focus may lead to an overindulgent style of parenting that puts the kids in control and you out of control along with your eating.

If your kids are in control, there are some things you can do. You can take parenting classes that center on boundaries and control issues. You can develop a set of rules and make your children aware of the correlating consequences when the rules are not followed.

You do not need to be held captive in your home at the mercy of your children. Regaining control is almost always painful. But it is never as difficult as living with children who do not respect you. If you are struggling because your children are taking all of your energy and leaving you so depressed that you think only about what you are going to eat next, make the changes that put you back in control.

GENTLE RELATIONSHIPS

Relationships are demanding. But you can't live without them. Maybe you eat because your relationships are so painful that you gently comfort yourself with food. Maybe your relationships are not obviously destructive, but you are linked to people who would rather have you overweight as a way of dealing with their own insecurity. Still other relationships are not completely unhealthy, but because of a life-style, you as the overeater are always being put in places where you are highly vulnerable and the temptation is strong.

> *Make your life and body priorities.*

Whatever the case for your relationships, you must see your life and your body as priorities. You must make good and tough decisions that will surround you with gentle and comforting people who want you to succeed.

The Prayer of a Gentle Eater

Dear God, help me heal my relationships. Help me make tough decisions so that people around me will be gentle with me. Help me love these people as You love me. Thank You for the opportunity to love and the ability to choose.

Chapter 12

Accountability

Detachment is my mode. I don't get too close to people.
Then when I want to move on, it's not that hard. I'm
afraid for anyone to get close to me, where I really live.
I don't want that. I don't want to finally reveal who I
really am, only to have that part of me turned away. And
I don't want to have to answer to anyone. If I want to
be irresponsible, I don't want to have another mother
figure or father figure reminding me I'm not measuring
up, I'm a failure, and I have to do better. I expect so
much of myself and fall so short of my expectations. All
I need is one more person to expect something of me that
I can't deliver.

—A Fellow Struggler

BREAKING THE DETACHMENT MODE

Accountability is something we all need, but most of us do not want to go through the pain of experiencing it. We prefer to run free with no one to answer to. We have been shamed so often by others that we don't want to set up a relationship that will leave us feeling worse about ourselves. For us, it is time to see where our detachment mode has led us. It is time to stop long enough to comprehend the influence of our style on our inability to control our weight. We need others to help us if we are finally going to succeed.

Accountability can come in many varieties. If you are married, you need to be accountable to your spouse. But if you are married and having trouble losing weight, the last person you want to be accountable to is a spouse. Your spouse is most likely going to be too harsh or too easy with you. And so many other aspects of your relationship can get confused with the eating problem that you will probably do better to find accountability outside your marriage—especially with someone of the same sex.

Step 10: Find a person or group to hold you accountable for making healthy decisions.

In an accountability relationship, you have someone to share your plans with, someone to hear your plans and provide encouragement for you to achieve them. This person gently confronts you when you don't stick to your plan. Choosing the right person (or persons) is important to your success.

SEEKING SOMEONE TO HELP

Perhaps the best person to work with is someone who has had a weight problem and has been successful in keeping off the pounds for a long period of time. This person has adopted a whole new life-style and is succeeding in it. The wisdom and experience can be of great benefit to you and motivate you when you get discouraged.

The best form of accountability is a small group of people, all of whom have overcome personal difficulties and habits that were ruining their lives and relationships. The small group is superior because it offers different perspectives on your problems.

Many programs are designed to offer you accountability. The diet programs advertised on television often talk of a counselor to help you. That counselor is a paid source of accountability.

Weight Watchers features a time for sharing progress with each other. Knowing you are going to return next week and provide an update to everyone can motivate you toward your goals.

Overeaters Anonymous (OA), patterned after Alcoholics Anonymous, is structured around accountability. When you show up, you are expected to be open and honest about your problems. One feature of affiliating with and working the OA program is finding a sponsor. Your sponsor is your primary source of accountability and makes a commitment to you to be available when needed.

I must issue one warning about accountability groups. They are very easy places to fake it. You can't fake it completely, but you can fake it enough to turn the group into something destructive. You do that by revealing just enough to make people think you are being real and open and vulnerable while you are actually hiding the real issues troubling you. I have been in groups where superficial sharing allowed attendees to fake it. They looked so good going to the group each week, but group attendance only provided a cover for their irresponsible behavior.

If you cannot find a sponsor or a group, you may want to pay for an accountability relationship. Many counselors who specialize in eating problems can help you resolve your problems while holding you accountable. Paying for counseling may motivate you to be more honest to ensure you are getting your money's worth.

You need help. Eventually, you will love it. You will find yourself growing and maturing. Accountability can cost you your old behaviors and open you up to a new world in which you are in control.

The Prayer of a Gentle Eater

Dear God, help me do what I fear the most. Help me be accountable to someone on this earth. It is so much easier to just be accountable to You. Having to answer to real flesh and blood is not so easy. Guide me to a person who can encourage me when I need it and gently confront me if I must be confronted. Help me grow through being accountable.

Chapter 13

Eating as an Addiction

I used to have a problem with food. Now the problem has me. It has me totally and completely. I want to change, but the moment I stop eating, I crave more food. I'm hooked. The more I attempt to do without food, the more food I want. I am overwhelmed by the urge to eat and eat again. Surely others are not so compelled to eat what they do not want. Surely others do not battle and lose the battle so consistently. If I could, I would stop it forever, but I cannot. I am not just hooked on food. I am hooked on thinking about food. It has become an overwhelming addiction.

—A Fellow Struggler

FROM DEPENDENCY TO ADDICTION

For some of us, food has become an addiction. It started out as a dependency but has moved into a fierce and raging addiction.

We need to consider the underlying issues that lead to the compulsive behavior. The issues of depression, control, self-esteem, abuse, and intimacy fuel the addiction. Until they are resolved, the addiction will have a life of its own.

It will grow in power until it eventually destroys you and some of those around you. If the symptoms listed below sound familiar, you must begin to address your problem for what it is, an addiction.

1. Continued Use in the Midst of Adverse Consequences

This is the hallmark of addiction. You misuse food to the point of death or the loss of everything but your life. Nothing is too bad to cause you to stop. You hear a spouse say, "I'm leaving," but it's not enough to make you stop. You hear a doctor say that your blood pressure is so high that a heart attack or stroke is inevitable, but it just doesn't have enough impact to cause you to change your behavior.

*Address your
food addiction.*

The severity of these problems and the lack of motivation to respond to them lead to the diagnosis of addiction. Addiction has power. It has the power to control everything you do and are. If your constant question is *why, why, why,* the answer could be addiction, addiction, addiction!

2. Larger Quantities Producing Less Satisfaction

For a drug addict, this is called tolerance. It takes more and more to do less and less. It is the law of diminishing returns. For a food addict, there is constant craving for the food that will provide the satisfaction and comfort to heal the anxiety or depression. The healing never comes, and the medication chosen to help only makes things much worse.

When I first started working with alcoholics, I was amazed at how much alcohol they could consume in one day. Some drank more than a case of beer in a day. Now, working with some overeaters, I am equally fascinated by their massive intake of calories. People wouldn't stuff themselves with that much food unless they were hooked with no other known means to survive.

If you eat far more than others can imagine, and they don't even know all that you eat because you hide half of it, you may be addicted to food.

3. Repeated Attempts to Stop

If you identify a problem and you are able to correct it, you move on and live a healthy life. But if you repeatedly try to stop eating incorrectly and you repeatedly fail, addiction to food has a strong grip on you.

4. Progression

Addiction problems always get worse when untreated. They never magically go away. Often the overeater prays for a quick fix or hopes that things will get better with the new year. They don't. They grow worse. The weight goes up, breathing becomes more labored, and life becomes more depressing. Family situations continue to fall apart, and work goes unrewarded. Just like the alcoholic, the food addict spirals downward into an abyss of despair and sometimes even to the point of death.

5. Withdrawal

Take away the drugs from a heroin addict, and the withdrawal process begins. The addict feels uncomfortable and edgy and often develops severe headaches and cramps. She seems miserable at every point. She craves more drugs, knowing that with one injection, all of the discomfort will go away.

I had a similar experience with food. The more intent I was on not overeating, the more I was drawn to forbidden food. I was nervous and irritable, and if I didn't find something all-consuming to do, I felt like I was going to go crazy. That is food addiction at its worst.

6. Shame

Addiction always ends in shame. You do what you do to feel better and experience relief, and yet you feel intense shame. How many times have you gorged yourself and then felt so guilty about how much you ate that you ate more? You felt like a worthless human being. It's the shame that most of us have experienced, and it's the shame that addicts of all kinds go through. Even when we stop eating out of control, sometimes the shame comes roaring back, and we relapse because the shame hooks us into our old patterns.

Shame is not the belief that you make mistakes; it is the deep sense that you *are* a mistake. It is a horrible feeling that you do not measure up and will not measure up. It turns the rejection of others into complete self-rejection.

THE WAY OUT OF ADDICTION

If you find that you are addicted to food, there are some things you can do to release the power of the addiction.

First of all, find a quiet place with no television or radio blaring. Attempt to write out what you see as your problems.

Then, share your list with someone, and ask for input. Are there areas you haven't addressed that are obvious to someone else? Humbling yourself before an objective friend or counselor may be a breakthrough experience that finally allows you to see the truth about yourself and the extent of your problems.

Next, learn to forgive those who have abused you and forgive yourself for abusing others. And accept God's forgiveness for all you have done to harm others. Of course, asking is not enough; believe you are forgiven and live as if you are forgiven.

> *Forgive yourself,*
> *and*
> *forgive others.*

Once you feel this forgiveness and give it to others, you can learn to love others and God and yourself again. Through this life-style of love, along with some accountable relationships, you can live free of addiction. You can turn your adversity into a new life mission full of the joy of helping others while you allow God to heal your wounds.

If you are addicted to food, no diet is going to help you. You will have to deal with food as an addiction and recover from that addiction the same way an alcoholic recovers from alcohol addiction. When you are determined to do that, you will be amazed at the freedom you feel.

The Prayer of a Gentle Eater

Dear God, I know this problem has me. I know I am dependent and out of control as an addict. In and of myself, there is no hope. But with You, there is. I can't handle this, God. You can, so I will let You. Here, take me and my addiction. For the first time, I am completely Yours.

Chapter 14

Relapse Prevention

I've been here before. I don't like being here, either. I hate it. I tried; I failed; I relapsed. And now I'm fatter than when I started. I'm more miserable than when I started. And I don't feel like getting started again. Maybe there is no way I can attain a healthy weight. My whole life is two steps forward and three steps back. What's the use if the only place I go is where I've always been?

—A Fellow Struggler

THE RELAPSE REALITY

What could be worse for people like us than to work so hard to lose weight only to discover that we lost ground and more of our self-esteem and more of our hope? Relapse is hard on all of us. We feel as if we have a mountain to climb that is too high and too rugged. At its essence, a permanent weight-loss program is a relapse prevention program that never stops.

Relapse is not gaining a pound or two or discontinuing regular amounts of weight loss. Relapse is going from long-term loss back to short-term and long-term gains. There will always be variations, and there will be times when your weight rises a little (five pounds or so), no matter how little or differently you eat. You must not allow one fluctuation to put you into a relapse mode, giving up the progress you have made.

HIGH-RISK SITUATIONS

High-risk situations pose a threat to long-term progress. Business meals and holidays are extremely high risks. A business meal may be stressful or boring. It's easy to get caught up in what others are ordering or so involved in the business agenda that you forget how much you are eating. During the holidays, you may be surrounded by every type of food you love—at parties, at the office, at restaurants, and so on. Whether it's a business meeting or a holiday gathering, you must start with a plan if you are going to succeed.

The plan should include thinking through the situation and developing nonfood or safe food alternatives. For instance, if you need something to do at a boring business meal, take notes. If you are going to a party, determine what you are going to drink (preferably water) and what foods you will eat a lot of and what foods you will taste. Once you have your plan, stick to it. When you can't stick to it, leave the party. When you have victory in high-stress situations, you'll feel more confident in other circumstances, too.

SAFE RESTAURANTS

Eating out can be frustrating, even if it's for pleasure. One of the worst decisions I can make is to go to a Mexican restaurant where the service is slow-paced and the baskets of chips are plentiful. I can eat a full day's worth of fat grams and more in the thirty minutes I wait for the food. Mexican restaurants with high-fat chips are not safe places for me and my waistline. However, even if a Mexican restaurant is unsafe for you now, someday you'll be able to eat in one because you'll eat the amount of chips you want and no more. As long as you eat gently most of the time, you'll be okay.

The concept of safe places is vital for a relapse prevention program. For each person there are uniquely safe and unsafe restaurants from which to choose. Before you make a commitment to eat out, be sure your choice of restaurant offers safe and healthy foods. By refusing to eat somewhere, you may be considered a bit quirky, but at least you will be able to stay on your plan. If others cannot understand that need, you may question whether or not you would want to have dinner with them anyway.

Select restaurants serving healthy food.

Investigate the restaurants in your area. Go in and check out the menus for breakfast, lunch, or dinner. Look for the salad or low-calorie section, and ask questions about how the food is prepared and whether or not substitutions are acceptable.

One of my favorite restaurants is in Laguna Beach right on the ocean. I can hear the pounding surf as well as watch a great sunset. I work fairly close to it, and one day we took some people there for lunch. I ordered fish and asked

how it would be prepared. The waitress told me all their
fish was either fried or sautéed. I asked if they could broil
a piece for me. The answer was no. I asked if they could
steam or poach a piece. The answer was no. So I left.
Rather than sit there and eat something I didn't want, I left
my associates to finish their lunches. You need that kind of
resolve to stay on your plan. (By the way, I heard they now
broil fish at the restaurant. I may go back soon and give it
another try.)

I am committed to my plan, and I am committed to eating
whatever makes me feel good and healthy. Some foods that
I loved the most left me feeling tired and groggy. I didn't
like that feeling any more than I liked the concept that I
was on a diet. I don't use the *d* word, and I don't think you
should, either. It denotes a short-term plan to restrict food
that usually ends in a return to destructive eating habits.
Rather than diet, we prevent relapse by developing changes
and finding healthy places in which to implement those
changes, even in restaurants.

A favorite spot for an overweight overeater is a salad bar.
If you choose the salad bar, be educated in what foods really
contain. Select the lettuces, cucumbers, tomatoes, and
vegetables. Avoid the pasta salads, tuna salads, potato salads, and all the salads containing oil or mayonnaise. Those
items will turn your well-planned lunch into a high-fat and
high-calorie meal. Few salad bars provide a nonfat salad
dressing, so take your own. You can purchase salad dress-
ings in small packets or keep them refrigerated at your
workplace in small containers.

To enhance the flavor of your salad, use spices. You may
find these spices at some salad bars and not at others. Be
prepared with your own. No-salt varieties can add flavor to
your meal.

If you desire a piece of bread, have one. But don't put butter or margarine on it. Create a delicious alternative by dipping your bread in the nonfat salad dressing you are using and sprinkle some herbs and spices on top.

If soup is included with the salad, you may have to avoid it because of high sodium content. If it tastes salty, it is full of sodium, and if it has light round bubbles of oil floating on the top, it is high in fat. I have found that some specialty restaurants prepare some soups without the high level of sodium or fat content. If that is the case where you are eating, enjoy one of them.

FOOD AND THE MOOD

Keep in mind that not only is food content important for healthy, safe eating but so is the conversation content. If you are eating out with friends, avoid discussion that can lead to emotional topics. Such conversation can cause you to overeat to comfort yourself or release some pain or anger you might be experiencing. Light conversations complement light meals.

*Discuss pleasant
topics while
eating.*

If a major issue needs to be discussed, wait until you get home, out of the high-risk setting of a restaurant. There will be plenty of time for that type of discussion. You may even want to start the dinner by stating your desire to have a great time and not get too deep in conversation at the table. An uncomfortable assertion of your desires now may lead to a comfortable feeling when you look at yourself in the mirror in six months.

ASSERTING OURSELVES

Relapse often occurs when we know what to do, but for some reason, we aren't willing to assert ourselves to do it. At a party, someone offers us guacamole dip and chips and says it is a favorite recipe. We don't want to hurt the person's feelings so we have it and act like we love it—even if we are allergic to avocados. We feel rejected because we are overweight, and rather than risk temporary rejection, we set ourselves up to continue to be rejected. If we can break through that initial thought pattern and assert our need to say no, we will avert a relapse and feel a deep sense of accomplishment.

We need to stay in charge of our own destinies and not allow ourselves to be bullied into a relapse. We also need to identify all the places and conditions that set us up for failure. You will have your own list. Here are some of mine:

- Loneliness
- Boredom
- Depression
- Party
- Dinner with friends
- Stress
- Excitement of closing a deal
- Celebration of an accomplishment
- Holiday gatherings

Each situation allows me to be talked into unplanned eating or talk myself into it, so I am very cautious when I approach these times.

Those who don't relapse think well of themselves and believe they can accomplish their goals. They have hope, and they focus on all of the things they do right rather than obsess over all the things that do not go right.

If your self-talk is always negative, you will kill your efforts at change. If you blame yourself for everything and carry around a world of guilt, you can't help destroying your efforts at change.

THE PREDICTABLE PATTERN OF RELAPSE

Relapse has a predictable pattern that can be broken before it goes too far. First, there is *complacency*. You stop doing all the things that you know are helpful and healthy. Second, there is *confusion*. You wonder if your problem was really as bad as you thought. You convince yourself you have a new outlook that will allow you to handle any situation. Third, you *compromise*. You set yourself in too many high-risk situations to resist. Once you reach that stage, it is only a matter of time before the fourth stage, *catastrophe*, hits and you lose control.

You don't have to reach the fourth stage. You can intervene at any time. You can see the lack of effort, feel the confusion, and fight off the urge to compromise what you have worked so hard to build.

Everyone involved in a weight-loss program is going to struggle with occasional setbacks. The best way to handle a setback is to remember that you are working on a gentle lifetime approach to eating. The best gift that you can give yourself is grace. Remind yourself that tomorrow is a new day, and make the choice to get back on the path to healthier eating.

However, if you are slipping day after day, you would do well to find a counselor to help you discover what your relationship with food is all about. Oftentimes, underlying issues lead you to food for comfort. Pinpointing the issues is a comfort in itself. When you know the reason, you can stop beating yourself up and considering yourself a failure. Many counselors have struggled in this area themselves and are trained to help you with your new lifetime commitment.

The Prayer of a Gentle Eater

Dear God, help me protect myself from people and places that will set me back. Give me the courage to stand up for myself and my needs. Help me to see when I am slipping and to grab on to You before it is too late.

That's it! That is the gentle eating plan that has enabled me to shed excess pounds and the label *overweight*. It's a plan that you can implement and control. It has the elements needed to produce lasting change in the face of an often frustrating challenge. It isn't earth shattering, but it can be life changing if you are willing to make the gentle changes recommended.

Chapter 15

So You Want to Help Someone Else

You know, it seems like I married the wrong person. I can't even stand to hear him breathe. It's embarrassing how he dresses. His clothes are so tight, he looks like at any minute he might explode. There has to be more to life than this. I refuse to allow him to look this way. He has to change. If he doesn't, I don't know how much longer I can stand it. I need someone to help me.

—A Fellow Struggler

MAKING APPROPRIATE
DECISIONS ABOUT HELPING

Once we achieve something in our lives, we are reluctant to allow other people the same process we had to go through to take care of their problems. For instance, no one is more intolerant of a smoker than a former smoker. I know because I am one. How quickly we forget the complexities of finding a way out of the addiction.

Part of our problem is a sincere desire to help. However, if we act on the desire to help too soon, we will fail. If we start with the wrong motives, we will fail. If we are unbalanced in our lives, we will fail. We must take our time and not rush out to conquer the world or show the world that we have conquered our own problems.

The following guidelines may help if you want to be a good influence and an effective support to someone who finally wants to change.

1. What Worked for You May Not Work for Someone Else

Don't forget that God created all of us uniquely, and we all respond to different aspects of a weight-loss program in different ways. For some, the key becomes burning off an extra five hundred calories a day. For others, the key is eliminating five hundred calories by lowering their fat intake. Some need to begin a diet on a Monday. Others need to start on the first of the month. You need to encourage and support and give people the freedom to find their unique keys to the kingdom of a new body and a new attitude.

2. The Quickest Way to Relapse Is to Act Like an Expert

It takes time to go from being able to change to being wise. If you too soon act like an expert, you put yourself in a box. You become reluctant to share your struggles, and fairly soon you trip yourself up because you hide who you really are. The best thing to do is to lie low for a while and enjoy yourself. If what you have is real, it will last. You don't need to rush.

Keep yourself humble, and approach others from the perspective of a fellow struggler. Remind yourself that without the help of God, you would not have made it. See the real goal as long-term change for yourself. Part of your problem may be impatience, and not moving too quickly after you begin your recovery may require every ounce of patience you can muster.

3. Don't Take Responsibility for the Other Person's Eating Habits

If you are married or going with someone who is trying to change, you may feel responsible for the other person's eating habits. You may be tempted to walk on eggshells so as not to upset the person and trigger an eating binge. I'm sure you have seen people who are supposedly in love arguing in a restaurant over what to order or the fact that the other person isn't eating what is healthy.

Be a humble encourager.

You have to learn to take a deep breath and let it go. You have to learn to turn the person over to God. Don't give in to the temptation to believe that you have the power to change someone. You don't. And if you act like you do, the other person may do anything to ensure you understand how powerless you are.

4. Don't Look Over the Other Person's Shoulder

You know how annoying it is to have someone looking over your shoulder, analyzing everything you do. You must refrain from checking up on the person, adding fat grams for him, or throwing out the fattening food he buys. Freedom and hope motivate a person to change. If you give him room so he feels freedom, he is more likely to succeed. But if he feels trapped by two unrelenting eyes of judgment, he may rebel or sabotage his plans just to cause you pain.

Think of yourself as a humble helper. If you are on your knees trying to help someone, you can't be in a position to look over his shoulder. Commit yourself to becoming an encourager.

5. Be Gentle with the Person

As you know by now, I believe the key to long-term change is gentle, manageable change in an atmosphere of positive support. If your spouse is overweight and has caused you to miss out on many things in life, you may lose control and allow your bitterness to spew out onto her. You may feel a little better afterward, but it won't get you what you want and it won't help her stay on track.

This is a cruel world full of people who are often too busy to meet others' needs. We need more people who will slow down long enough to nurture and gently help others with their struggles. That is what you needed and still need today. Be sure you are getting enough counseling to keep your anger in check. If you aren't, obtain help for some old anger that continues to hamper your relationships so you can reflect the gentle behavior that benefited you when you needed it most.

6. Don't Judge Progress in the Midst of a Relapse

A friend was outraged to find her husband in the kitchen frying up a pound of bacon for himself. He had been working his program a couple of months, and it was too hard on him.

His reaction was like that of an alcoholic ordering a case of vodka. His wife was furious, even though she had done the same thing over and over on her way to a completely new shape.

If the person has had a problem for many years, relapse is almost inevitable. But relapse does not have to be a disaster. If handled well, it can be the beginning of permanent change. It can educate the person into some weak spots of his program. He can see his problems and start a new, more comprehensive program. If he is encouraged, there is a good chance he will pick up where he left off. If he is shamed, he is more likely to continue to eat, feeding the guilt that has arisen from the evaluation of failure. The degree of severity of the relapse has nothing to do with the eating program that will be reestablished. If you see someone frying up a pound of bacon, maybe you should look the other way until he has eaten all he can stand.

7. Don't Use a Favorite Food as a Reward

Just about the time someone gets used to living without a favorite food, another person comes along to tempt her with it. Never be the one to suggest or provide a food that has been a problem to someone else. If I had lost twenty pounds and someone had given me my two most tempting foods, I might have been lost forever. I can't turn down nachos, and I can't resist deep-fried onion rings. My mouth is watering just thinking about them. There are things that you could call trigger foods, and if you become the supplier, you may trigger a relapse that is difficult to turn around. Instead of offering your friend a previously favorite food, let her decide when to begin enjoying that food again (in moderation, of course).

8. Don't Eat Forbidden Foods in Front of the Person

Not only should you not provide someone with a favorite food, but it is even worse punishment for you to eat the food when you are around her. You don't have to alter your entire life, but you may want to make some small sacrifices. Family meals can offer good-tasting low-fat foods that will please everyone and still allow the person with the eating problem to feel satisfied. Some recovering overeaters could care less what you eat, but many more are fragile and need to be as free from temptation as possible.

9. Don't Leave Articles by the Bed

Heavy people are always receiving the latest diet book or an article on how people can become thinner. It frustrates the person, makes him angry, and provides another excuse to eat. If you have something you want to say, say it. If an article is important, discuss it. But don't leave messages lying around or taped to the bathroom mirror.

10. Praise Progress but Don't Lie

Anyone working on a weight problem wants to hear about noticeable progress. The temptation, though, is to flatter the person before the results are identifiable. When you see progress, mention it. If you don't see it, provide some other form of encouragement. Tell the person how hard it was for you to break through certain barriers. If you can't say something positive about the person's weight, find something in another area to praise. Gentle nurturing by thinking of the person's need to be recognized can help the person persevere through tempting times.

11. Don't Expect It to Last if You Do It for Someone Else

The person has to change because of a motivation for a better life for self, not someone else. External motivation works for the quick fix and short-term results. But when the person begins to work on herself for herself, sensing the value that God has placed on her, she can make real progress. Encourage the person not to say what sounds good or sacrificial; encourage her to realistically look at her situation and see the need for change for herself.

If you have maintained your weight loss, you must not forget how hard it was to come to that point when enough really was enough. If someone close to you needs you, be there for him. Help him and support him in every way possible, but keep your distance. You don't want to fall back into unhealthy habits if you spend too much time helping someone else and forgetting to manage your life.

Make someone else's struggle easier.

An unbalanced person trying to help someone else will always produce at least one disaster. A balanced person gently reaching out with love and understanding from the perspective of a fellow struggler can be a life-changing influence of unlimited value. If you do not reach out to someone to help, your weight loss was all for vanity. If you take your struggle and make someone else's easier, you have allowed God to increase the value of your life. When you hear someone say that she owes much of her success to you, you will be motivated to reach out and help others.

The Prayer of a Gentle Eater

Dear God, help me help someone else. Help me do it for all the right reasons. Love someone else and help someone else through me. Help me get out of this prison of self-obsession and carry this message of hope to others who need it.

If you would like to refer someone to a counselor, 1-800-NEW LIFE is staffed with caring professionals.

Section 2

THE GENTLE EATING COOKBOOK

A theme of this book is that there are a lot of healthy things you can do to help yourself without depriving yourself. Deprivation will provide you with the short-term results that never last. By eating better tasting food and better quality food, not less food, you will be able to achieve your personal goal of weight loss and become healthier at the same time.

We live in an exciting time because the food industry has made weight loss more manageable than it has ever been before. We now have available to us nonfat and low-fat and low-sugar food products that are absolutely delicious. These items, if properly selected, will help us gently change from foods that we *were* eating to foods that will nurture us. Keep in mind that this one accomplishment of changing the way you eat can be the foundation for changing the way you live and the satisfaction you get from living.

The three of us who worked on this book are living examples of a gentle eating life-style. Each of us has maintained a weight loss of at least twenty-five pounds for over ten years, beating all the odds against long-term weight loss. We did it because we were tired of the old way, and we did it by eating smarter while being gentle with ourselves.

One of our goals is to teach you about the gentle eating method, which involves new ways of cooking and shopping so that everyone in your family can be part of the system. In our fast-paced society, you need to learn to cook for the on-the-go life-style. If you don't, you will be tempted to eat too often at fast-food places that don't honor your need for healthy food. To be successful, you need to know the right times and the wrong times to cook. For instance, don't cook when you are craving food; your frequent tasting might add many calories and fat grams to your diet without you knowing. You also need to know when you should shop for food and when it is unsafe to shop. As a whole, the method takes your present resources and helps you adapt them to your everyday life-style without compromising healthy eating and living.

Chapter 16

Let's Go Shopping

Shopping for groceries is a procedure that can help you with your plan if you are willing to educate yourself about what you are buying. Reading the label is the only way to know if the item is something you want for yourself and/or your family. Some of the lowest fat content items contain the highest sodium and cholesterol content, which defeats the healthy purpose. Some foods labeled "no cholesterol" have the highest concentrations of fat. And some foods that appear to be healthy, such as granola, can have excessive amounts of fat, sodium, sugar, and cholesterol.

Once you start reading packaging information, you will become an avid reader. For me, it becomes a game. It is as if I am looking for treasure, and when I find something I want, I win big. One night my wife and I were talking about how long it had been since we had a really good and satisfying thick and chewy pizza. The next day I was determined to go into the store, read all the labels, and find a way to make a low-fat or a nonfat pizza. First, I found some nonfat round pieces of dough that could pass as pizza dough. Then, I discovered a nonfat cheese, and next, I discovered a pizza tomato sauce made with no fat. I bought fresh mushrooms, went home, and made my wife a pizza that I would put up against anyone's fancy store-bought kind.

PREPACKAGED PRECAUTIONS

Be especially cautious with prepackaged food. Many prepackaged, frozen, low-calorie meals are loaded with sodium, which makes you retain water. The portion size of the meals is also much smaller than that in the recipes in this section. When I look at the portions of these meals in the grocery store, I get the feeling of deprivation. Small portions are not necessarily the sign of healthy eating. If you are looking for the convenience of prepackaged meals, you can cook on the weekend or in the evenings and freeze them for later use. Not all prepackaged food is undesirable, and it seems to be getting better every day. The caution for all of us is to read the label before we buy and then consider how much food there was and whether or not we felt satisfied after we ate it.

CREATIVITY

One key to an ongoing successful plan is your creativity. When you shop, think of a favorite food, and try to find something that will substitute for it, like my pizza discovery. If you are creative, you can do something similar with every other food. If you are a Mexican food lover, you can find nonfat refried beans, nonfat tortillas, and all sorts of other items you love. There are even baked nonfat chips that can be eaten with nonfat salsa. Use your mind. Create what you want to eat, and then search for the products that will turn your favorite foods into healthy choices.

SAFE SHOPPING

When you head for the grocery store, be sure you go when it is safe, that is, when your stomach is satisfied.

Shopping for food when you are hungry or in a hurry can be dangerous. This condition may cause you to automatically spot out the old, quick, fattening foods you used to eat. Take a list of foods you need to buy. Seek out the items on your list, and refuse to buy impulse things.

When I go to the store, the safest place is the produce section. Other than an avocado, it's hard to go wrong with almost anything there. Instead of a cabinet full of junk food, I now have a basket full of fresh fruit. Every morning my daughter eats a banana and I eat an apple. It is now part of our life-style. Fresh vegetables taste so much better than frozen or canned ones. And it isn't that much more difficult or time-consuming to prepare the fresh rather than the packaged kind. Produce departments are located right next to the flowers and plants. If your budget allows, buy yourself a beautiful bouquet of flowers occasionally to set the nurturing tone for your shopping experience.

Shopping can be an important part of the foundation of a long-term program for change. The problem comes when emotions cause you to react in an unplanned manner. If you are upset, angry, lonely, or sad, try to hold off going grocery shopping so that your emotions won't affect your selections and the quality or quantity you buy. Go with the attitude that you are doing something truly worthwhile for yourself, your family, and the future.

Once you decide to do your grocery shopping on purpose and according to your plan, you need some help. The following information comes from foods available at most grocery stores. We found them while we were doing our treasure hunt–style shopping. It's so exciting to see how many good and healthy food products are available to us if we just look for them. We do not endorse any of the items listed, nor do we endorse any particular grocery store. This list is merely a guide.

SHOPPING GUIDE

Item	Qty.	Cal.	Sod.	Fat	Chol.
Cheeses					
Alpine Lace Mozzarella	1 oz	40	290 mg	0	5 mg
Alpine Lace Cheddar	1 oz	40	290 mg	0	5 mg
Alpine Lace Monterey Jack	1 oz	40	290 mg	0	5 mg
Healthy Choice Monterey Jack	1 oz	40	200 mg	0	5 mg
Healthy Choice Mozzarella	1 oz	40	200 mg	0	5 mg
Healthy Choice Mozzarella Cheese Sticks	1 oz	30	200 mg	0	5 mg
Healthy Choice Cream Cheese	1 oz	24	170 mg	0	5 mg
Philadelphia Cream Cheese	1 oz	30	180 mg	0	5 mg
Alpine Lace Cream Cheese	1 oz	30	180 mg	0	0
Smart Beat Cheddar Cheese Slices	1 slice	40	380 mg	0	5 mg
Borden Swiss Cheese Slices	1 slice	40	380 mg	0	5 mg
Borden Sharp Cheddar Cheese Slices	1 slice	40	260 mg	1 g	5 mg
Alpine Lace Cheddar Cheese Slices	1 slice	40	260 mg	0	5 mg
Milk					
Nonfat	8 oz	90	130 mg	0	NL
Alta Dena	1 oz	35	35 mg	2 g	NL
Knudsen Free					
Sour Cream	1 Tbsp	18	20 mg	0	NL
Smart Beat Vegetable					
Spread/Butter	1 Tbsp	20	105 mg	2 g	0
Knudsen Cottage Cheese	4 oz	70	300 mg	0	5 mg

NL = not listed

Item	Qty.	Cal.	Sod.	Fat	Chol.
Coffeemate	1 Tbsp	10	10 mg	1 g	0
Glen Oaks Yogurt Drink					
Ultra Light	8 oz	132	95 mg	0	NL
Strawberry	8 oz	132	95 mg	0	NL
Raspberry	8 oz	132	95 mg	0	NL
Tropical Fruit	8 oz	132	95 mg	0	NL
Stoney Free Yogurt Drink					
Wild Blueberry	8 oz	150	115 mg	0	0
Tropical Fruit	8 oz	150	115 mg	0	0
Cappuccino	8 oz	150	115 mg	0	0
Apricot Mango	8 oz	150	115 mg	0	0
Nonfat Yogurt					
Alta Dena Peach Nonfat Yogurt	8 oz	190	128 mg	0	0
Alta Dena Vanilla Nonfat Yogurt	8 oz	190	128 mg	0	0
Alta Dena Blueberry Nonfat Yogurt	8 oz	190	128 mg	0	0
Alta Dena Cherry Nonfat Yogurt	8 oz	190	128 mg	0	0
Alta Dena Strawberry Nonfat Yogurt	8 oz	190	128 mg	0	0
Alta Dena Mixed Berries Nonfat Yogurt	8 oz	190	128 mg	0	0
Dannon Cherry Nonfat Yogurt	8 oz	100	150 mg	0	5 mg
Dannon Vanilla Nonfat Yogurt	8 oz	100	150 mg	0	5 mg
Dannon Blueberry Nonfat Yogurt	8 oz	100	150 mg	0	5 mg
Dannon Peach Nonfat Yogurt	8 oz	100	150 mg	0	5 mg
Dannon Lemon Chiffon Nonfat Yogurt	8 oz	100	150 mg	0	5 mg
Knudsen Free Strawberry Yogurt	6 oz	170	130 mg	0	5 mg

Item	Qty.	Cal.	Sod.	Fat	Chol.
Nonfat Yogurt *(cont'd)*					
Knudsen Free Vanilla Yogurt	6 oz	170	140 mg	0	5 mg
Knudsen Free Blueberry Yogurt	6 oz	170	130 mg	0	5 mg
Knudsen Free Red Raspberry Yogurt	6 oz	170	130 mg	0	5 mg
Yogi Nonfat Peachy Peach Yogurt	5.6 oz	50	63 mg	0	0
Yogi Nonfat Blue Cheese Cake Yogurt	5.6 oz	50	63 mg	0	0
Yogi Nonfat Cherry Vanilla Yogurt	5.6 oz	50	63 mg	0	0
Pudding					
Hershey Free Chocolate Pudding	4 oz	100	200 mg	0	5 mg
Frozen Desserts					
Dreyers Pralines & Cream Ice Cream	4 oz	130	70 mg	2 g	5 mg
Dreyers Nonfat Vanilla Ice Cream	4 oz	90	65 mg	0	0
Dreyers Nonfat Chocolate Ice Cream	4 oz	100	40 mg	3 g	10 mg
Dreyers Nonfat Raspberry Ice Cream	4 oz	100	35 mg	3 g	10 mg
Meats					
Zacky Farms Turkey Strips	3 oz	300	0	3 g	0
Armour Boneless Turkey Strips	3 oz	90	20 mg	1 g	0
Healthy Choice Ground Beef	4 oz	130	240 mg	4 g	55 mg
Louis Rich Oven Roasted Turkey	1 oz	25	290 mg	1 g	10 mg
Jimmy Dean Light Sausage (turkey and pork)	2 oz	80	230 mg	7 g	25 mg

Item	Qty.	Cal.	Sod.	Fat	Chol.
Armour Turkey Bacon	1 strip	30	170 mg	2 g	15 mg
Mr. Turkey Bacon	1 strip	30	110 mg	2 g	0
Lunch Meats					
Healthy Choice Bologna	1 slice	10	100 mg	2 g	5 mg
Healthy Choice Chicken Breast	1 slice	10	90 mg	2 g	5 mg
Healthy Choice Honey Ham	1 slice	10	80 mg	2 g	5 mg
Healthy Choice Turkey Breast	1slice	25	210 mg	1 g	10 mg
Healthy Choice Bunsize Franks	1 frank	70	570 mg	2 g	20 mg
Galileo Turkey Breast	1 slice	10	100 mg	<1 g	0
Galileo Honey Ham	1 slice	10	90 mg	<1 g	0
Healthy Favorites Boiled Ham	1 slice	4	115 mg	<1 g	5 mg
Healthy Favorites Turkey Breast	1 slice	12	100 mg	<1 g	5 mg
Soups					
Health Valley Chicken Broth	7.5 oz	20	290 mg	1 g	100 mg
Health Valley 5 Bean Vegetable Soup	7.5 oz	100	260 mg	1 g	100 mg
Health Valley Vegetable Barley Soup	7.5 oz	120	270 mg	3.2 g	100 mg
Health Valley Minestrone Soup	7.5 oz	80	270 mg	3.2 g	100 mg
Health Valley Tomato Vegetable Soup	7.5 oz	50	290 mg	1.6 g	100 mg
Health Valley Mild Vegetarian Chili	5 oz	140	290 mg	1 g	0
Health Valley Spicy Vegetarian Chili	5 oz	140	290 mg	1 g	0
Pasta					
De Bolg's Angel Hair Pasta	2 oz	210	3 mg	1 g	0

Item	Qty.	Cal.	Sod.	Fat	Chol.
Pasta *(cont'd)*					
De Bolg's Tomato & Basil Pasta	2 oz	200	8 mg	1 g	0
De Bolg's Garlic & Parsley Pasta	2 oz	200	8 mg	1 g	0
De Bolg's Rotini	2 oz	200	8 mg	1 g	0
No-Yolks Noodles	2 oz	210	18 mg	1 g	0
Pasta Sauce					
Healthy Choice Pasta Sauce	4 oz	40	350 mg	1 g	0
Healthy Choice Garlic & Herbs	4 oz	40	350 mg	1 g	0
Healthy Choice Pasta Sauce (with mushrooms)	4 oz	40	350 mg	1 g	0
Healthy Choice Garlic & Onions	4 oz	40	350 mg	1 g	0
Canned Goods					
Apple Time Applesauce	4 oz	50	50 mg	0	0
Del Monte Sliced Peaches	½ c	60	0	0	0
Del Monte Apricot Halves	½ c	60	0	0	0
Del Monte French Style Green Beans	½ c	10	10 mg	0	0
Libby's Lite Fruit Cocktail	½ c	50	10 mg	0	0
S & W Garbanzo Beans	½ c	110	235 mg	1 g	0
S & W Ready Cut Peeled Tomatoes	½ c	25	20 mg	0	0
Store Brand Diced Tomatoes in Tomato Juice	½ c	25	170 mg	0	0
Bumble Bee Tuna (in water)	¼ c	60	250 mg	1 g	NL
Star Kist Tuna (in water)	¼ c	60	250 mg	<1 g	NL
Salad Dressings					
Kraft Fat Free Mayonnaise	1 Tbsp	8	125 mg	0	0

Item	Qty.	Cal.	Sod.	Fat	Chol.
Seven Seas Red Wine Vinegar	1 Tbsp	6	190 mg	0	0
Seven Seas Ranch	1 Tbsp	20	125 mg	0	0
Seven Seas Italian	1 Tbsp	4	220 mg	0	0
Healthy Sensation Thousand Island	1 Tbsp	20	135 mg	0	0
Healthy Sensation Ranch	1 Tbsp	16	140 mg	0	0
Healthy Sensation Honey Dijon	1 Tbsp	25	140 mg	0	0
Healthy Sensation Italian	1 Tbsp	16	140 mg	0	0
Bernsteins Cheese Fantastico	1 Tbsp	32	160 mg	2 g	4 mg
Bernsteins Creamy Dill	1 Tbsp	16	150 mg	1 g	0
Bernsteins Oriental	1 Tbsp	25	150 mg	1 g	0
Hidden Valley Italian Parmesan	1 Tbsp	16	140 mg	0	0
Hidden Valley Honey Dijon	1 Tbsp	16	140 mg	1 g	0
Good Seasons Spice Packets					
Italian	1 Tbsp	6	170 mg	0	0
Creamy Italian	1 Tbsp	6	135 mg	0	0
Honey Mustard	1 Tbsp	10	130 mg	0	0
Zesty Herb	1 Tbsp	6	150 mg	0	0
Syrup					
Aunt Jemima Syrup	2 Tbsp	100	90 mg	0	0
Mrs. Butterworth's	2 Tbsp	60	65 mg	0	0
Pancakes					
Aunt Jemima Pancakes	3–4 in	230	610 mg	2 g	10 mg
Hungry Jack Pancakes	3–4 in	180	660 mg	2 g	5 mg
Cake Mixes					
Pillsbury White Cake	1/12 of cake	180	310 mg	3 g	35 mg
Pillsbury Yellow Cake	1/12 of cake	180	310 mg	3 g	35 mg
Devil's Food Super Moist Cake	1/12 of cake	190	330 mg	3 g	0
Betty Crocker Yellow Cake	1/12 of cake	190	330 mg	3 g	0

Item	Qty.	Cal.	Sod.	Fat	Chol.
Frosting					
Betty Crocker Chocolate Frosting	1/12 of cake	130	50 mg	1 g	0
Betty Crocker Vanilla Frosting	1/12 of cake	130	50 mg	1 g	0
Pillsbury Lovin Lites Chocolate Frosting	1/12 of cake	130	95 mg	2 g	0
Pillsbury Lovin Lites Fudge Frosting	1/12 of cake	130	95 mg	2 g	0
Pillsbury Lovin Lites Vanilla Frosting	1/12 of cake	130	95 mg	2 g	0
Wesson Lite Cooking Spray	.27 g	0	0	0	20 mg
PAM Cooking Spray	.26 g	2	0	1 g	0
Popcorn					
Orville Redenbacher's Butter Flavor	3 c	60	310 mg	2 g	0
Jiffy Pop	3 c	80	230 mg	2 g	0
Rice Cakes					
Quaker Natural Rice Cakes	1 cake	35	35 mg	1 g	0
Quaker White Cheddar Rice Cakes	1 cake	35	35 mg	1 g	0
Hain Mini Regular Rice Cakes	1/2 oz	60	40 mg	1 g	0
Hain Mini Mild Cheddar Rice Cakes	1/2 oz	60	70 mg	1 g	0
Hain Mini Apple Cinnamon Rice Cakes	1/2 oz	60	15 mg	1 g	0
Hain Mini Honey Nut Rice Cakes	1/2 oz	60	30 mg	1 g	0
Hain Mini Caramel Rice Cakes	1/2 oz	60	15 mg	1 g	0
Crackers					
Mr. Phipps Crackers	8 crackers	60	200 mg	1 g	0
Nabisco Wheat Crackers	5 crackers	50	160 mg	0	0

Item	Qty.	Cal.	Sod.	Fat	Chol.
Pretzels					
Mister Salty Pretzel Sticks	1 oz	100	380 mg	0	0
Eagle Pretzel Sticks	1 oz	110	570 mg	2 g	0
Sourdough Hard Pretzels	1 oz	110	570 mg	0	0
Granola					
Health Valley Tropical Fruit	1 oz	90	20 mg	1 g	0
Health Valley Raisin Cinnamon	1 oz	90	35 mg	1 g	0
Health Valley Date & Almond	1 oz	90	20 mg	1 g	0
Muffins					
Betty Crocker Light Wild Blueberry Muffin Mix	1 oz	90	140 mg	1 g	20 mg
Health Valley Multi Bran Muffin Mix	1 oz	140	100 mg	0	0
Health Valley Banana Muffin Mix	1 oz	140	100 mg	0	0
Health Valley Raisin Spice Muffin Mix	1 oz	140	100 mg	0	0
Cookies					
Health Valley Raisin Apple	1 cookie	80	80 mg	0	0
Health Valley Raspberry	1 cookie	80	80 mg	0	0
Health Valley Apple Fruit	1 cookie	80	80 mg	0	0
Health Valley Date Fruit	1 cookie	70	35 mg	0	0
Health Valley Tropical Fruit	1 cookie	90	45 mg	3 g	0
Health Valley Apricot Delight	1 cookie	90	45 mg	3 g	0
Fig Newton Apple	1 cookie	70	45 mg	0	0
Cereal					
Health Valley Organic Bran	1 oz	90	10 mg	0	0
Health Valley Oat Bran	1.2 oz	100	30 mg	1 g	0

Item	Qty.	Cal.	Sod.	Fat	Chol.
Cereal *(cont'd)*					
Health Valley Corn Puffs	1 oz	100	45 mg	1 g	0
Health Valley Cinnamon Apple	1 oz	100	45 mg	1 g	0
Fruit Bars					
Health Valley Apricot Fruit Bars	1 bar	140	10 mg	<1 g	0
Health Valley Date Fruit Bars	1 bar	140	10 mg	<1 g	0
Health Valley Raisin Fruit Bars	1 bar	140	10 mg	<1 g	0
Desserts					
Entenmanns Cinnamon Rolls	1 bun	130	110 mg	0	0
Entenmanns Fudge Brownies	1 slice	110	170 mg	0	0
Entenmanns Cookies	2 cookies	80	105 mg	0	0
Entenmanns Cake	1 oz	70	95 mg	0	0
Entenmanns Coffee Cookies	1 cookie	80	95 mg	0	0

A new line of low-fat, low-calorie foods is called Just Help Yourself. It offers a wide selection of low-sodium breakfasts, lunches, and dinners under three hundred calories with no more than three grams of fat per one hundred calories. Here are some of the items:

Breakfast
   Sausage Omelet Muffin Sandwiches
   Buttermilk Pancakes
   Omelets and Hash Browns

Lunch
   Chicken Fajitas
   Chicken Chow Mein

Macaroni and Cheese
Chicken Primavera

Dinner
Salisbury Steak
Shrimp and Pasta Marinara
Chicken Enchiladas
Homestyle Pot Roast
Chicken Italiano
Sirloin Beef Tips
Roasted Chicken with Gravy
Sweet and Sour Chicken
Beef Pepper Steak
Chicken with Barbecue Sauce

Another very healthy line of foods is called Healthy Choice. It has a variety of low-sodium, low-fat, and low-cholesterol foods under three hundred calories as well:

Breakfast
Eggs—frozen

Lunch
Glazed Chicken
Macaroni and Beef
Macaroni and Cheese
Turkey with Vegetables
Beef and Bean Burritos
Chicken Enchiladas
Chicken Fajitas
Lasagna

Dinner
Meatloaf Dinner
Beef Sirloin Tips

Pasta Classics
Southwestern Chicken Dinner
Breast of Turkey Dinner
Mesquite Chicken Dinner
Breaded Fish Fillets and Sticks
Turkey Tetrazini
Teriyaki Chicken

From all of these selections, anyone should be able to find nutritious food that is low in fat, sodium, cholesterol, and sugar. When you see so many selections, it is hard to imagine why anyone would take a path of deprivation over a path of nutritious eating. As I said earlier, due to this type of variety, it has never been easier to lose weight. Now it is up to you to find treasures at the grocery. Then you will be ready to put it all together with the recipes in the following chapters.

Chapter 17

Breakfast Recipes

These breakfast recipes will be satisfying to your entire family. Teaching your children at an early age how to eat healthy food will help them make healthy choices as adults. All of these recipes taste as good as higher-fat recipes, yet they are much better for you. We suggest combining some of the breakfast recipes with the lunch recipes for a healthy, satisfying brunch.

OAT BRAN MUFFINS

Nonstick cooking spray
1 tsp vanilla extract
1 tsp almond extract (or second tsp vanilla)
2 Tbsp vegetable oil
$1/4$ c honey
$3/4$ c skim milk
4 large egg whites, lightly beaten
$1/4$ tsp salt (optional)
1 Tbsp baking powder
$1/4$ c raisins (or currants)
$1/4$ c chopped unsalted nuts
$1/4$ c brown sugar, firmly packed
$2 1/2$ c oat bran, uncooked

Preheat oven to 350°.

In a bowl, combine oat bran, sugar, nuts, currants, baking powder, and salt. Mix well.

In a small bowl, combine egg whites, milk, honey, vegetable oil, and almond and vanilla extracts. Add to dry ingredients and mix to blend.

Spray 2 muffin tins lightly with cooking spray, or use paper muffin cups. Bake 20 to 25 minutes or until light brown. Serve warm or at room temperature. Yield: 12 muffins.

Contents per muffin:

> *Calories: 155*
> *Sodium: 161 mg*
> *Fat: 5 g*
> *Percentage of fat to calories: 27 percent*
> *Cholesterol: .3 mg*

COCOA MUFFINS _____

³/₄ c whole wheat flour
³/₄ c all-purpose flour
¹/₂ c sugar
1 Tbsp baking powder
1 Tbsp unsweetened cocoa powder
1 tsp ground cinnamon
¹/₄ tsp salt or salt substitute (optional)
1¹/₂ c All-Bran cereal
1¹/₂ c skim milk
2 egg whites
2 Tbsp vegetable oil
Nonstick cooking spray

Stir together flours, sugar, baking powder, cocoa, cinnamon, and salt or salt substitute. Set aside.

Measure All-Bran cereal and milk into a large mixing bowl. Let it stand 3 minutes or until cereal is softened. Add egg whites and oil. Beat well.

Add flour mixture, stirring only until combined. Spoon batter evenly into 12 muffin pan cups (2½ inches in diameter) coated with cooking spray.

Bake at 400° about 22 minutes or until lightly browned. Serve warm. Yield: 12 muffins.

Contents per muffin:

> *Calories: 221*
> *Sodium: 276 mg*
> *Fat: 6.7 g*
> *Percentage of fat to calories: 13 percent*
> *Cholesterol: .5 mg*

FRENCH TOAST

3 large egg whites, lightly beaten
6 slices cinnamon raisin bread
Nonstick cooking spray
2 Tbsp apple-almond butter

Place egg whites in a medium pie plate. Place 2 slices of bread into pie plate and let soak 5 to 10 seconds. Turn bread over another 5 to 10 seconds. Remove from plate and set aside. Repeat with the remaining slices of bread.

Coat a nonstick skillet with cooking spray. Heat the skillet over medium high heat. When the skillet is hot, add the prepared slices of bread. Brown the slices evenly on both sides.

Serve with a teaspoonful of apple-almond butter on each slice of bread. Yield: 3 servings.

Contents per serving:

> *Calories: 223*
> *Sodium: 244 mg*
> *Fat: 8.3 g*
> *Percentage of fat to calories: 33 percent*
> *Cholesterol: 0 mg*

BREAKFAST TOAST

> **2 slices whole wheat bread**
> **1 tsp vegetable oil**
> **1/2 tsp nonfat "butter" granules**
> **Ground cinnamon to taste (optional)**

Preheat broiler. Lightly toast bread. Brush 1 side of each slice with oil, and sprinkle with "butter" (side up). Toast again 30 to 60 seconds or until nicely browned. Sprinkle with cinnamon. Yield: 1 serving.

Contents per serving:

> *Calories: 187*
> *Sodium: 358 mg*
> *Fat: 8 g*
> *Percentage of fat to calories: 33 percent*
> *Cholesterol: 0 mg*

BROCCOLI, CHEESE, AND SUBSTITUTE EGG OMELET

1/4 c egg substitute
1/4 c broccoli
1 oz nonfat cheddar cheese
Nonstick cooking spray
2 Tbsp diced onions (optional)
2 pinches salt (or salt substitute)
3 pinches garlic powder

Combine the egg substitute, broccoli, onions, salt substitute, and garlic. Whip them together with a fork until the texture is smooth.

Coat an 8-inch skillet with cooking spray. Set your stove top on medium low, and add the already combined ingredients. Cover with a lid.

Using an egg turner, slightly rotate it around the edges, so the omelet will not stick to the sides of the skillet. As the omelet thickens, sprinkle the cheese evenly over it. Using the egg turner again, circle around the edges of the pan. When the texture has reached a soft yet solid form, take the egg turner and edge it halfway around and in the middle of the omelet, then fold it in half. Cook it for approximately 1 to 2 more minutes, then slide onto a plate. Yield: 1 serving.

Contents per serving:

  Calories: 112.75
  Sodium: 901.7 mg
  Fat: 2.2 g
  Percentage of fat to calories: 18 percent
  Cholesterol: 5.8 mg

CINNAMON ROLLS

1 c skim milk
3 Tbsp sugar
3 Tbsp margarine
1 package dry yeast
1/4 c warm water (105° to 115°)
1 egg, beaten
1/2 tsp salt
3 3/4 c and 2 Tbsp bread flour
Nonstick cooking spray
1/4 c plus 2 Tbsp firmly packed brown
    sugar
1 Tbsp skim milk
1/2 tsp vanilla extract
2 Tbsp ground cinnamon
3 Tbsp powdered sugar

Heat milk over medium high heat in a heavy saucepan to 180° or until tiny bubbles form around the edge. Do not boil. Remove from heat.

Add sugar and 1 tablespoon margarine, stirring until margarine melts. Let cook until warm (105° to 115°).

Dissolve yeast in warm water in a large bowl. Let stand 5 minutes. Add milk mixture, egg, and salt. Stir well.

Gradually stir in 3½ cups of flour to make a soft dough. Turn out onto a lightly floured surface, and knead until smooth and elastic, about 8 minutes. Add flour, 1 tablespoon at a time, to keep dough from sticking to the surface.

Place the dough in a large bowl coated with cooking spray. Cover and let rise in a warm place that is free from drafts. Allow the dough to rise until it is double in bulk.

Punch down the dough. Turn out onto a lightly floured surface. Roll into a 20-by-8-inch rectangle. Brush 2 tablespoons melted margarine over the entire surface. Sprinkle brown sugar and cinnamon evenly over dough.

Beginning at the lowest side, roll dough up tightly, pinching the seam to seal. Do not seal the ends of the roll.

Cut the roll into 20 1-inch slices. Arrange slices in a pan coated with cooking spray. Cover and let rise in a warm place approximately 30 minutes.

Bake at 350° for 22 minutes. Combine powdered sugar, milk, and vanilla; stir well. Glaze mixture over rolls. Yield: 20 rolls.

Contents per roll:

> *Calories: 127*
> *Sodium: 88.7 mg*
> *Fat: 2.7 g*
> *Percentage of fat to calories: 19 percent*
> *Cholesterol: 10.9 mg*

HOMEMADE OATMEAL

¹/₃ c rolled oats
³/₄ c water
Salt
Brown sugar
Cinnamon
Skim milk

Combine oats and water in a 2-cup glass measure. (Make sure the measurement is correct to keep the oatmeal from boiling up and spilling over.) Microwave on high for 2½ minutes. Then let stand 1 minute. Add brown sugar, cinnamon, and milk to taste. You could use a nonsugar sweetener instead of sugar. Also, you might want to add raisins or figs to your oatmeal. Yield: 1 serving.

Contents per serving:

Calories: 103
Sodium: 1 mg
Fat: 2 mg
Cholesterol: 0

CHEESY HASH BROWNS

2 peeled potatoes
2 Tbsp onions
¼ c red pepper
3 sprinkles garlic powder
Nonstick cooking spray
2 oz nonfat cheddar cheese
2 pinches salt (or salt substitute)

Grate the 2 peeled potatoes, and combine them with the onions, red pepper, garlic powder, and salt substitute.

Coat a saucepan with the cooking spray. Add the combined ingredients to the slightly heated pan, and cook at medium high.

Continuously stir and toss ingredients. After the potatoes are softened, wait until cooked and slightly browned, then sprinkle the cheese. Reduce the heat to low, and cover the pan for approximately 1 or 2 minutes until cheese is melted. Remove from the heat and serve. Yield: 3 servings.

Contents per serving:

Calories: 106.4
Sodium: 433.8 mg
Fat: .1 g
Percentage of fat to calories: 2 percent
Cholesterol: 5 mg

PANCAKES

1 extra-large egg
1 egg white
1¼ c skim milk
¼ tsp vanilla extract
¹⁄₁₆ tsp salt (or salt substitute)
¹⁄₁₆ tsp ground nutmeg
1 heaping c unbleached white or whole
   wheat flour
1 heaping tsp baking powder
Nonstick cooking spray

Beat egg and egg white lightly in blender jar or in a bowl. Add milk, vanilla, salt or salt substitute, nutmeg, flour, and baking powder. Beat briefly. A few lumps will remain.

Let batter sit a few minutes before using. Pour batter in ¼ cup portions onto a nonstick griddle lightly coated with a cooking spray, and cook until golden brown on both sides. Yield: 4 servings.

Contents per serving of 3 pancakes:

Calories: 178
Sodium: 176 mg
Fat: 2.1 g

Percentage of fat to calories: 10 percent
Cholesterol: 54.5 mg

For topping suggestions, review the "Shopping Guide" to low-fat and nonfat items. Try a low-fat syrup, sliced fruit, nonfat yogurt, or sugar-free and fruit-only spread toppings.

BANANA-ORANGE SHAKE _____

> 1 c orange juice
> 1 small ripe banana
> 1/4 c instant nonfat milk powder
> 1/2 c ice cubes
> 1/4 c club soda

In a blender, process orange juice, banana, milk powder, and ice cubes until mixture is thick and ice cubes are crushed. Add club soda, stir, and serve immediately. Yield: 1 serving.

Contents per serving:

> *Calories: 82.8*
> *Sodium: 57 mg*
> *Fat: 2.7 g*
> *Percentage of fat to calories: 28 percent*
> *Cholesterol: 4.7 mg*

YOGURT FRUIT CUP _____

> 1 16-oz can sliced peaches or pears,
>   packed in fruit juice
> 16 oz low-fat vanilla yogurt

2 Tbsp finely chopped almonds
1/2 tsp ground cardamom

Drain and divide fruit among 6 small bowls. Top with the yogurt and sprinkle lightly with nuts and cardamom. Serve immediately. Yield: 6 servings.

Contents per serving:

Calories: 278
Sodium: 144.3 mg
Fat: .8 g
Percentage of fat to calories: 3 percent
Cholesterol: 3 mg

MELON WITH SHERBET

1 small honeydew melon, cut in half and
  seeded
2 oranges and 1 c strawberries
2 Tbsp confectioners' sugar, sifted
12 oz rainbow sherbet (6 2-oz scoops)

With a melon baller, scoop out flesh of the melon. Section oranges and slice strawberries. Combine melon, oranges, and strawberries in a bowl, and chill.

Place confectioners' sugar in a pie plate. Dampen the rims of 6 small glass bowls, and dip the rims individually in confectioners' sugar.

Divide the fruit mixture among bowls; top each with a scoop of sherbet. Serve immediately. Yield: 6 servings.

Contents per serving:

> *Calories: 156*
> *Sodium: 37.5 mg*
> *Fat: 1.4 g*
> *Percentage of fat to calories: 8 percent*
> *Cholesterol: 4.1 mg*

SAUSAGE BISCUIT SANDWICHES _____

1 8-oz package low-fat turkey smoked sausage
2 10-oz cans refrigerated buttermilk flaky biscuits
¼ c honey or barbecue sauce (optional)

Preheat oven to 400°.

Cut the sausage lengthwise in half; cut each half into 5 pieces. Remove biscuits from the can, and separate. Using fingers, flatten each biscuit to a 4-inch diameter.

Place small amount of honey or barbecue sauce, if desired, in the center of each biscuit. Top each with 1 piece of sausage. Bring up the edges of the biscuit, and pinch together to seal over the top of the sausage. Place on a baking sheet; bake about 10 minutes or until lightly browned. Yield: 20 small sandwiches.

Another option: approximately 2 minutes before the biscuits are ready, sprinkle a pinch of nonfat cheese, and cook until melted.

Contents per sandwich:

> *Calories: 91.1*
> *Sodium: 241 mg*

Fat: 5.5 g
Percentage of fat to calories: 55 percent
Cholesterol: 9.5 mg

This recipe contains a high portion of sodium per small biscuit. Use this recipe for special occasions. Or if you use it on a more frequent basis, watch your sodium intake for the rest of the day. It would be wise to select a low-sodium lunch and dinner.

SPICY CINNAMON MUFFINS _____

1½ c all-purpose flour
½ c sugar
2 tsp baking powder
½ tsp salt
½ tsp ground nutmeg
½ tsp ground coriander
½ tsp ground allspice
½ c low-fat milk
⅓ c margarine, melted
1 egg
¼ c sugar
1 tsp ground cinnamon
¼ c margarine, melted

Preheat oven to 400°.

Grease 36 miniature muffin cups. In a large bowl, combine flour, ½ cup sugar, baking powder, salt, nutmeg, coriander, and allspice.

In a small bowl, combine milk, ⅓ cup margarine, and egg. Stir into flour mixture just until moistened. Spoon batter into muffin cups. Bake 10 to 13 minutes or until edges are lightly browned and/or a wooden pick inserted in the center comes out clean. Remove from pan.

Meanwhile, combine remaining ¼ cup sugar and cinnamon in a shallow dish. Roll warm muffin tops in ¼ cup melted margarine. Then roll them in sugar-cinnamon mixture. Serve while warm. Yield: 36 mini-muffins.

Contents per muffin:

> *Calories: 77.7*
> *Sodium: 91.6 mg*
> *Fat: 3.2 g*
> *Percentage of fat to calories: 36 percent*
> *Cholesterol: 6 mg*

RICE CREPES _____

- 1 8-oz carton egg substitute
- ⅔ c evaporated skim milk
- 1 Tbsp margarine, melted
- ½ c all-purpose flour
- 1 Tbsp granulated sugar
- 1 c cooked rice (white or brown)
- Nonstick cooking spray
- 2 c canned or 2½ c fresh fruit (strawberries, raspberries, blueberries, or another favorite fruit)
- 10 tsp low-sugar or no-sugar fruit spread
- 10 tsp low-fat sour cream or nonfat sour cream substitute
- 1 Tbsp confectioners' sugar for garnish (optional)

Combine egg substitute, milk, and margarine in a small bowl. Stir in the flour and granulated sugar until smooth and well blended. Stir in rice. Let stand 5 minutes. Heat 8-inch nonstick skillet or crepe pan. Coat with the cooking spray.

Spoon batter into pan. Lift pan off the heat. Quickly tilt the pan in a rotating motion so that the bottom is completely covered with the batter. Place pan back on the heat, and continue cooking until surface is dry, about 45 seconds. Turn crepe over, and cook 15 to 20 seconds. Set aside. Continue with remaining crepe batter. Place waxed paper between crepes.

Spread each crepe with your favorite filling: strawberries, raspberries, blueberries, fruit spread, or sour cream. Roll up, and sprinkle with confectioners' sugar for garnish. Yield: 10 crepes.

Contents per crepe (excluding confectioners' sugar):

> *Calories: 135*
> *Sodium: 91.1 mg*
> *Fat: 4.5 g*
> *Percentage of fat to calories: 29 percent*
> *Cholesterol: .9 mg*

BRAN BUNS

1 c 100% bran, divided
⅓ c firmly packed light brown sugar
¼ c diet margarine, melted
1 apple, cored and sliced
2 c buttermilk baking mix
1 c water
¼ c egg substitute

Preheat oven to 450°.

In a small bowl, combine ¼ cup bran, brown sugar, and margarine. Spread in an 8-by-8-by-2-inch pan. Top with the apple slices and set aside.

In a medium bowl, combine baking mix, remaining ¾ cup bran, water, and egg substitute until soft dough forms. Drop dough by ¼ cupfuls over the apple slices. Bake for 13 to 15 minutes or until done. Invert onto a heatproof plate, leaving pan over buns for 2 to 3 minutes. Cool slightly. Serve warm. Yield: 9 buns.

Contents per bun:

> *Calories: 194*
> *Sodium: 435 mg*
> *Fat: 6.7 g*
> *Percentage of fat to calories: 30 percent*
> *Cholesterol: .1 mg*

Chapter 18

Lunch or Brunch Recipes

Almost all of the recipes in this chapter can be altered with different spices and added nonfat or low-fat items. By being creative, you will soon find out how exciting and adventurous it is to come up with your own recipes. You will see that these recipes not only will be delicious but will help you reduce your weight as well.

VEGETABLE MEDLEY

> 1 c frozen brussels sprouts
> 1 c frozen tiny whole carrots
> ¼ c water
> 2 Tbsp nonfat Italian salad dressing

Combine brussels sprouts and carrots, and steam them until they are soft. (Be careful not to overcook your vegetables because you'll steam out the valuable nutrients.) Drain the vegetables, and return them to a saucepan. Add the salad dressing, and toss to coat. Cook 1 minute more or until heated through. Yield: 2 servings.

Contents per serving:

Calories: 112
Sodium: 224 mg
Fat: 1.8 g

Percentage of fat to calories: 14 percent
Cholesterol: 1 mg

With this recipe, you can add more items or change the vegetable variety by using the "Shopping Guide" and adding the calories, sodium, fat, and cholesterol listed for each item. This recipe would be great with yolkless pasta. Also adding additional spices and diced red and green peppers would provide extra flavor. This meal can be frozen overnight and defrosted during the day. You may eat it cold from your cooler while on the road or at the office.

CABBAGE AND TOMATO TOSSED SALAD

Dressing
  1/4 c sugar
  1/2 tsp salt
  1/4 tsp celery seed
  3 Tbsp cider vinegar

Salad
  4 c torn lettuce
  1 c shredded napa, savoy, or green
    cabbage
  1 large tomato, cut into thin wedges

In a small bowl, combine all the dressing ingredients. Blend well. In a large bowl, combine all the salad ingredients. Just before serving, pour dressing over salad. Toss the salad so that the dressing is spread evenly. Yield: 4 servings.

Contents per serving:

Calories: 63.4
Sodium: 279 mg

Fat: .2 g
Percentage of fat to calories: 3 percent
Cholesterol: 0

With this recipe, you can add different foods or spices to complement your salad. For example, you could broil a 3-ounce skinless chicken breast (calories: 140.4; sodium: 62.3 mg; fat: 3 g; percentage of fat to calories: 21 percent; cholesterol: 72.2 mg), slice it into small pieces, and toss them into the salad. Another idea would be to shred ½ ounce nonfat mozzarella or cheddar cheese (calories: 72.9; sodium: 133.7 mg; fat: 4.6 g; percentage of fat to calories: 57 percent; cholesterol: 16.2 mg) on top and toss it in. You might want to add fresh garlic and/or vegetables to this salad. All of these suggestions are easy to do and will still keep this recipe low in fat, sodium, calories, and cholesterol.

ORANGE GLAZED BABY CARROTS ___

½ c water
1 c frozen baby whole carrots
2 Tbsp fresh orange juice
½ tsp cornstarch
1 tsp chopped fresh chives
⅛ to ¼ tsp grated orange peel, if desired

Bring the water to a boil in a small saucepan. Add carrots. Return to a boil, and stir. Reduce the heat, cover, and simmer 4 to 7 minutes or until crisp yet tender. Then drain. In a small bowl, combine orange juice and cornstarch. Stir until smooth. Add orange juice mixture, chives, and orange peel to carrots. Cook and stir 1 to 3 minutes. Yield: 1 serving (or 2 if you serve another item with it).

Contents per serving:

Calories: 83
Sodium: 88.1 mg
Fat: 0
Percentage of fat to calories: 0 percent
Cholesterol: 0

With this recipe, you could have a baked potato with 1 tablespoon of low-fat margarine and 2 large pinches of shredded cheddar, Swiss, or Monterey Jack nonfat cheese (calories: 306.5; sodium: 212.8 mg; fat: 8.2 g; percentage of fat to calories: 24 percent; cholesterol: 8.1 mg).

Another side selection could be 1 cup steamed vegetables with 1 teaspoon nonfat ranch dressing and ½ ounce low-fat cheese on top (calories: 154.4; sodium: 307.8 mg; fat: 3.6 g; percentage of fat to calories: 19 percent; cholesterol: 12.1 mg).

If meat is your preference, broil a 3-ounce low-fat ground turkey burger loaded with your favorite spice and 1 egg white (calories: 150; sodium: 109.1 mg; fat: 2.7 g; percentage of fat to calories: 17 percent; cholesterol: 58.9 mg).

Another selection could be oven-baked french fries. Take 1 potato, and slice it into small french fry sizes. Coat a roasting pan with a nonstick cooking spray. Sprinkle on top with garlic powder and onion powder, and bake at 350° until they are browned and soft (calories: 223; sodium: 16.2 mg; fat: .2 g; percentage of fat to calories: 1 percent; cholesterol: 0). You can dip them into a nonfat dressing of your choice from your grocery list (calories: 10; sodium: 177 mg; fat: 1 g; percentage of fat to calories: 69 percent; cholesterol: 4 mg). A nonfat selection of cheese can be melted on right before pulling them from the oven (calories: 72.9; sodium:

133.7 mg; fat: 4.6 g; percentage of fat to calories: 57 percent; cholesterol: 16.2 mg). Or you may want to dip them in a nonfat sour cream substitute added with your favorite spices for flavor (calories: 59; sodium: 29 mg; fat: 5.5 g; percentage of fat to calories: 83 percent; cholesterol: 0).

VEGETABLE AND TURKEY STIR-FRY

    1 Tbsp oil
    1 turkey breast, thinly sliced (about ¾ lb)
    1 16-oz package frozen broccoli, carrots,
        water chestnuts, and red pepper
    1 medium onion, cut into thin wedges
    ¼ c prepared low-sodium stir-fry sauce
    3 c hot cooked rice

Heat a large nonstick skillet or wok over medium high heat until hot. Add oil. Heat until it ripples. Add turkey and cook. Stir 4 to 5 minutes or until no longer pink. Add frozen vegetables and onion. Cook and stir 6 to 8 minutes or until vegetables are crisp yet tender. Add stir-fry sauce. Cook until thoroughly heated. Serve over hot cooked rice. Yield: 4 1¼-cup servings.

Contents per serving:

    Calories: 525
    Sodium: 109.3 mg
    Fat: 4.5 g
    Percentage of fat to calories: 8 percent
    Cholesterol: 71.8 mg

With this recipe, you can also use fresh vegetables or put in another combination of vegetables. In all the recipes, the authors suggest that you use brown rice instead of white rice. It is higher in protein and fiber.

This is a perfect recipe to make in the evening or on the weekend. You may want to freeze it in 4 portions in freezer bags. That way you can take your already prepared lunch to the office and reheat it in the microwave. Again, if you choose, you can add any additional spices as long as you do not use salt. (Salt substitutes are fine. You may want to test them on a small portion of your meal, however, to get used to the taste.)

BEEF STIR-FRY SALAD _____

> 2 Tbsp lime juice
> $\frac{1}{2}$ lb top round steak, trimmed of all
>   visible fat, cut into very thin strips
> 1$\frac{1}{2}$ c thinly sliced red onion separated
>   into rings
> 1 medium green pepper, cut into thin
>   rings
> $\frac{1}{4}$ c chopped fresh cilantro
> $\frac{1}{2}$ c salsa
> 1 8-oz can kidney beans, drained
> 1 large tomato, coarsely chopped
> 3 c chopped lettuce
> Nonstick cooking spray

In a medium bowl, drizzle lime juice over steak. Coat a large nonstick skillet or wok with cooking spray. Heat over medium high heat until hot. Add beef with lime juice. Cook and stir for 2 to 3 minutes or until beef is no longer pink. Add onion and green pepper. Cook and stir for 3 to 4 minutes until vegetables are crisp yet tender. Add cilantro, salsa, and kidney beans. Cook and stir until thoroughly heated. Remove from heat. Stir in tomato. Serve over the lettuce. Yield: 4 servings.

Contents per serving:

Calories: 163.4
Sodium: 329.2 mg
Fat: 3.4 g
Percentage of fat to calories: 18 percent
Cholesterol: 27.9 mg

This recipe can be prepared in advance and frozen overnight, ready to take to the office or wherever you will be eating your lunch. Do not add the lettuce until you are ready to eat.

FOUR-BEAN SALAD

3/4 c thinly sliced purple onion
1 clove garlic, minced
2 Tbsp water
15 oz canned garbanzo beans, rinsed and
   drained
1 1/2 c fresh green beans, cut into thirds
8 oz canned black beans, rinsed and
   drained
8 oz canned kidney beans, rinsed and
   drained
1/3 c cider vinegar
1 tsp olive oil
1/4 tsp dry mustard
1 1/2 Tbsp sugar
3 carrots, thinly sliced
1/2 c chopped sweet red pepper

In a large microwavable casserole dish, combine onion, garlic, and water. Microwave on high for 1 to 2 minutes. Stir in all remaining ingredients except carrots and red pepper. Microwave on high for an additional 3 to 5 minutes or until the green beans are tender, yet crisp. Stir in carrots and red pepper. Serve immediately, or cover, refrigerate, and serve it cold. Yield: 9 servings.

Contents per serving:

Calories: 138
Sodium: 280 mg
Fat: 1.7 g
Percentage of fat to calories: 11 percent
Cholesterol: 0

ORIENTAL CHICKEN-PASTA SALAD ____

Salad
  **8 boneless, skinless chicken breast
    halves (about 1½ lb)**
  9 oz (3⅓ c) uncooked rotini (spiral) pasta
  **16 oz (4 c) fresh pea pods, trimmed and
    blanched**
  1 c diagonally sliced green onions
  **1 8-oz can sliced water chestnuts,
    drained and chilled**
  **2 11-oz cans mandarin orange
    segments, drained and chilled**

Dressing
  1⅓ c low-fat plain yogurt
  ¾ c reduced fat or nonfat mayonnaise
  2 Tbsp low-sodium soy sauce
  2 tsp cooking sherry or fruit juice

¼ to ½ tsp ginger
¼ tsp pepper

Place the chicken breast halves in a large skillet. Add just enough cold water to cover the chicken. Bring to a boil. Reduce the heat. Cover and simmer 14 to 20 minutes or until chicken is fork tender and juices run clear. Cool and cut chicken into cubes.

Meanwhile, cook rotini to desired texture as directed on the package. Drain and rinse with cold water. In a large bowl, combine rotini, pea pods, onions, water chestnuts, and cooked chicken.

In a small bowl, combine all dressing ingredients. Blend well. Pour dressing over salad mixture. Toss lightly to coat. Fold in mandarin orange segments. Yield: 10 ½-cup servings.

Contents per serving:

Calories: 270
Sodium: 105 mg
Fat: 4.9 g
Percentage of fat to calories: 16 percent
Cholesterol: 33.1 mg

COLESLAW WITH FRUIT _____

Salad
   1 8-oz can pineapple chunks (juice
      packed)
   2 c shredded cabbage
   ⅔ c chopped apple
   ½ c shredded carrot
   ¼ c chopped green pepper

Dressing
    1 Tbsp vegetable oil
    1 Tbsp honey
    1 Tbsp lemon juice
    $\frac{1}{8}$ tsp ground ginger
    $\frac{1}{8}$ tsp salt

Drain the pineapple chunks, reserving 2 tablespoons juice. Set juice aside.

For the salad, in a large bowl, combine pineapple, cabbage, apple, carrot, and green pepper.

For the dressing, combine in a screwtop jar the reserved pineapple juice, oil, honey, lemon juice, ginger, and salt. Cover and shake well.

Pour dressing over the salad. Toss lightly to coat. Chill 4 to 24 hours. Toss before serving. Yield: 4 servings.

Contents per serving:

> *Calories: 114*
> *Sodium: 80.9 mg*
> *Fat: 3.7 g*
> *Percentage of fat to calories: 27 percent*
> *Cholesterol: 0*

This recipe is one to remember for the holidays and can be used to re-create your old holiday meals into new traditions.

For lunch, you might add a broiled or barbecued skinless chicken breast, a low-fat turkey burger, or a broiled piece of fish with lemon on top.

This is another recipe that can be packed in your cooler. If you have a meeting with a client with whom you have built a relationship, offer to prepare a basket lunch for two!

TURKEY FAJITAS

1 medium green pepper, cut into thin
   strips
1 medium onion, sliced
2 Tbsp water
³/₄ lb cooked low-fat turkey, cut into thin
   strips (2 c)
¹/₃ c chunky salsa
1 Tbsp lime juice
¹/₂ tsp chili powder
8 7- to 8-inch flour tortillas
¹/₂ c chopped tomatoes
¹/₄ c imitation or light sour cream,
   if desired

In a 2-quart microwave-safe casserole, combine green pepper, onion, and water. Cover tightly. Microwave on high for 4 to 6 minutes or until crisp and tender. Stir once halfway through cooking and drain. Add the turkey, salsa, lime juice, and chili powder. Mix well. Cover. Microwave on high for 2 to 4 minutes or until thoroughly heated.

Wrap the tortillas in a microwave-safe plastic wrap. Microwave on high for 45 to 60 seconds or until warm.

Place about ¹/₂ cup turkey mixture in the center of each tortilla. Fold top and bottom edges of tortillas toward center. Fold sides toward center, slightly overlapping. Place on serving platter. Top each fajita with tomato and sour cream. Yield: 8 fajitas.

Contents per serving:

> *Calories: 197*
> *Sodium: 76.2 mg*
> *Fat: 5.2 g*
> *Percentage of fat to calories: 24 percent*
> *Cholesterol: 35.4 mg*

As a side dish to this recipe, combine cooked rice with salsa, chili powder, diced green and red pepper, garlic powder, and a Mexican nonsalt spice mixture (found in the spice rack at your grocery store). Mix all the ingredients together for delicious Spanish rice.

CREAM OF BROCCOLI SOUP

> 1 16-oz bag frozen cut broccoli, or use
>   fresh broccoli
> 1 small onion, diced
> 3 c water
> 1 Tbsp Gifford's basic spice
> 2 tsp low-sodium chicken bouillon
>   granules
> ¼ tsp Gifford's dessert spice
> 1½ Tbsp cornstarch, mixed with ⅓ c cold
>   water
> 1 c evaporated skim milk
> 2 Tbsp Worcestershire sauce

In a medium-size saucepan, combine the broccoli, onion, water, basic spice, bouillon granules, and dessert spice. Bring to a boil. Reduce the heat and simmer for 15 minutes.

Add the cornstarch mixture, slowly stirring constantly until mixture thickens. Reduce heat to low. Add milk and Worces-

tershire sauce. Stir and cook an additional 5 minutes. Yield:
4 servings.

Contents per serving:

> *Calories: 108*
> *Sodium: 178 mg*
> *Fat: .6 g*
> *Percentage of fat to calories: 5 percent*
> *Cholesterol: 2.6 mg*

THE FOLLOWING SALAD IDEAS GO
WITH THE CREAM OF BROCCOLI SOUP

VEGETABLE GARDEN SALAD _____

Combine 1 cup lettuce, ¼ cup carrots, 2 tablespoons celery,
½ cup tomatoes, ¼ cup cucumbers, 1 tablespoon onions,
¼ cup sprouts, and one hard-boiled egg with the yolk removed. Add 1 tablespoon of your favorite nonfat, low-sodium
salad dressing, and toss until the salad is coated.

> *Calories: 69.8*
> *Sodium: 266 mg*
> *Fat: 1.4 g*
> *Percentage of fat to calories: 17 percent*
> *Cholesterol: 4 mg*

CHARBROILED CHICKEN SALAD _____

Combine an assortment of ¼ cup pea pods, 2 teaspoons
water chestnuts, ¼ cup sprouts, and ½ cup tomatoes with
3 ounces charbroiled skinless chicken breast chopped into

bite-size pieces. Place your ingredients over 1 cup of the lettuce of your choice or a combination of your lettuce favorites. Mix in your favorite spices and 1 tablespoon of your selection of nonfat, low-sodium salad dressing, and toss until your salad is evenly coated.

> *Calories: 203.8*
> *Sodium: 253.5 mg*
> *Fat: 4.4 g*
> *Percentage of fat to calories: 20 percent*
> *Cholesterol: 76.2 mg*

TUNA SALAD DELIGHT

If you are a tuna lover, you'll love this one! Toss ½ can water-packed tuna with ½ cup tomatoes, 2 tablespoons celery, 2 tablespoons onion, and ¼ cup cucumbers, and add your favorite spice combination. Add 1 tablespoon nonfat mayonnaise. Slice 1 large tomato so that it opens like a tulip, and stuff your salad ingredients into its center.

> *Calories: 174.5*
> *Sodium: 539.3 mg*
> *Fat: 3.6 g*
> *Percentage of fat to calories: 18 percent*
> *Cholesterol: 39 mg*

SHRIMP SALAD

For a tasty shrimp salad, toss ½ cup tomatoes, ¼ cup cucumbers, 2 tablespoons onion, ¼ cup sprouts, and 3 ounces cooked and shelled shrimp. Add the spices of your choice and 1 tablespoon nonfat, low-sodium dressing, and place the mixture on 1 cup of lettuce.

Calories: 144.2
Sodium: 332 mg
Fat: 3.1 g
Percentage of fat to calories: 19 percent
Cholesterol: 151.5 mg

FRUIT SALAD

If you enjoy fruit, slice ¼ cup strawberries, ¼ cup orange sections, ¼ cup pineapple, ¼ cup honeydew melon, ¼ cup apples, and 1 tablespoon raisins. Place the fruit mixture on 1 cup of lettuce and top with ½ cup of your favorite nonfat yogurt.

Calories: 191.8
Sodium: 98.5 mg
Fat: 1 g
Percentage of fat to calories: 4 percent
Cholesterol: 2 mg

SPINACH SALAD

If you like spinach salad, mix together ½ cup fresh spinach leaves with ½ cup regular or romaine lettuce. Add ¼ cup orange slices and the spices of your choice. Slice two hard-boiled egg whites (egg yolks contain the fat and unwanted calories; egg whites contain the protein and low-fat calories). Top your salad with 1 tablespoon nonfat, low-sodium Italian dressing. Toss until the salad is evenly coated.

Calories: 80.6
Sodium: 252.5 mg
Fat: 1.7 g
Percentage of fat to calories: 19 percent
Cholesterol: 1 mg

STEAMED VEGETABLE PLATE _____

Combine 2 cups of your favorite vegetables in a steamer, and steam until cooked. (Do not overcook.) Sprinkle on 1 ounce of your favorite nonfat cheese and 1 tablespoon nonfat, low-sodium ranch or cucumber dressing. Spice to your desired taste, and you can enjoy a nonfat nutritious meal.

Calories: 271
Sodium: 735 mg
Fat: 0
Percentage of fat to calories: 5 percent
Cholesterol: 9 mg

Chapter 19

Appetizers and Snacks

An appetizer or a snack makes a great meal for one person, or you can combine a few together to make a family meal. A table full of these appetizers and snacks is great for a shower, a Super Bowl party, or any kind of celebration. After your guests comment on the taste of these goodies, you can let them know what healthy snacks they've been eating.

SALSA DIP

$3^1/_2$ c whole peeled tomatoes, cut up, with the juice
1 c low-sodium Contadina tomato sauce
1 c or 1 large finely chopped onion
$^1/_3$ c chopped green pepper
$^1/_3$ c or 4-oz can diced green chilies, drained
2 Tbsp chopped fresh cilantro
1 large garlic clove, crushed
$^1/_2$ tsp cumin
$^1/_2$ tsp salt
$^1/_4$ tsp black pepper

Combine tomatoes and juice with remaining ingredients in a large bowl. Refrigerate thoroughly. Yield: 5 cups.

For salsa and chips, you can purchase no-salt chips with less fat at your grocery store. However, salsa is not only for chips. Salsa is also great on a baked potato with melted nonfat cheese.

Add to the salsa nonfat, low-sodium ranch dressing, and place the mixture in the center of a vegetable tray. Include baby carrots, celery, cucumbers, tomatoes, and broccoli. Sprinkle with a mixture of garlic and herb nonsalt spices, and serve.

Add 2 teaspoons jalapeno peppers for hot salsa or 1 teaspoon for medium taste. This recipe for salsa is mild.

Contents per ¼ cup serving:

Calories: 50.1
Sodium: 234 mg
Fat: .3 g
Percentage of fat to calories: 5 percent
Cholesterol: 0

ARTICHOKE DIP

- ½ c low-fat sour cream
- ½ c processed low-fat or nonfat cream cheese
- ¼ c French's creamy mustard
- 1 9-oz package frozen artichoke hearts, thawed and finely chopped
- ½ c finely chopped red and green sweet peppers
- 1 tsp chili powder
- 2 Tbsp sliced green onions

To microwave, combine sour cream, cream cheese, and creamy mustard in a 1-quart microwavable bowl. Stir in artichokes, peppers, and chili powder. Cover the bowl with microwave-safe waxed paper.

Microwave on high for 5 minutes or until hot. Stir halfway through cooking.

Garnish with green onions. Serve with a chopped vegetable assortment. Yield: 5 servings.

Contents per serving:

> *Calories: 140*
> *Sodium: 234 mg*
> *Fat: 5 g*
> *Percentage of fat to calories: 46 percent*
> *Cholesterol: 0*

If you use the nonfat cream cheese, the fat content will be slightly lower.

NACHO CHEESE DIP

1 can vegetarian nonfat chili
1 c shredded low-fat cheese

Place the chili in a microwave-safe bowl. Heat on high for 1 minute until hot. Add the cheese, and stir it in until it is evenly mixed. Microwave on high for 1 minute or until the cheese is completely melted.

This recipe is a good dip for the oven-baked french fries. If you desire to make a meal out of it, add 2 cups yolkless pasta. If you prefer chips, you can find nonfat, no-salt chips at specialty stores in your area. (See product labels for nutrient information.)

BUTTERMILK HERB DIP AND VEGGIE TRAY

1/4 c buttermilk
1 8-oz carton reduced-calorie sour cream
2 Tbsp chopped fresh parsley
1/2 tsp dill weed
1/4 tsp salt or salt substitute
1/8 tsp black pepper
1/4 tsp minced fresh garlic
Fresh vegetable sticks

In a medium bowl, stir together all the ingredients, except the vegetable sticks. Cover and refrigerate until flavors are well blended (about 2 hours). Serve with the vegetable sticks or vegetable selection of your choice. Yield: 1 1/4 cups.

Contents per tablespoon:

Calories: 21.5
Sodium: 41.7 mg
Fat: 1.9 g
Percentage of fat to calories: 78 percent
Cholesterol: .1 mg

MINI-PIZZAS

1 6-oz can no-salt-added tomato paste
1 tsp dried oregano leaves
1 11-oz can whole kernel corn with red and green peppers, drained
1 2 1/4-oz can sliced ripe olives, drained
3 oz or 3/4 c nonfat mozzarella cheese
5 English muffins, halved

In a small nonmetal bowl, combine tomato paste and oregano. Blend well. Cover and refrigerate tomato paste mixture. Cover and refrigerate the corn, olives, and cheese in separate containers. Use within 3 to 4 days.

To assemble your mini-pizza, spread 1 muffin half with 2 tablespoons tomato paste mixture, 1 tablespoon corn, and 1 teaspoon cheese. Sprinkle 1 tablespoon olives over cheese. Place on a cookie sheet, and bake at 350° approximately 7 to 10 minutes. Keep a close eye on it, and remove when the cheese is melted and the muffin is browned. Yield: 10 pizzas.

Contents per pizza:

Calories: 245.9
Sodium: 860 mg
Fat: 1.7 g
Percentage of fat to calories: 13 percent
Cholesterol: 5 mg

You can add other spices or sprinkle with nonfat Parmesan cheese for extra flavor.

STUFFED MUSHROOMS

18 large mushrooms
1 Tbsp olive oil
1/4 c minced onion
1 clove garlic, minced
1 shredded wheat biscuit, crushed
1 Tbsp grated Parmesan cheese
1/2 tsp herb seasoning
Freshly ground black pepper to taste
1/2 tsp paprika

Preheat oven to 350°.

Clean the mushrooms with a vegetable brush. Remove and finely chop stems. Heat oil in a nonstick skillet over medium high heat. Sauté chopped mushroom stems, onion, and garlic until the onion is tender, 4 to 5 minutes. Remove from the heat. Stir in the shredded wheat, Parmesan cheese, herb seasoning, and pepper. Stuff the mushroom caps, packing the mixture firmly. Arrange the mushrooms in a shallow baking dish. Sprinkle the tops with paprika. Bake 20 to 25 minutes or until mushrooms are tender. Yield: 6 servings (3 mushrooms per serving).

Contents per serving:

> *Calories: 45.1*
> *Sodium: 20.3 mg*
> *Fat: 2.7 g*
> *Percentage of fat to calories: 51 percent*
> *Cholesterol: .8 mg*

This is another excellent appetizer for the holidays or special party occasions to replace a high-fat appetizer.

CHEESE-RICE CAKE SNACK

2 rice cakes, unsalted
1 tsp prepared yellow mustard
¼ c low-fat mozzarella (or Cheddar)
**   cheese (grated)**

Preheat oven to 350°.

Put the rice cakes on a baking sheet or aluminum foil, and bake 3 to 4 minutes or until crisp. Remove from the oven, spread with mustard, and top with cheese. Return to oven, and bake 3 to 4 minutes or just until cheese melts.

Serve immediately. Yield: 2 servings.

Contents per rice cake:

> *Calories: 74*
> *Sodium: 99.7 mg*
> *Fat: 2.6 g*
> *Percentage of fat to calories: 32 percent*
> *Cholesterol: 8.1 mg*

For an appetizer, replace the larger rice cakes with saltless mini-rice cakes.

BAKED POTATO SKINS

6 large Idaho potatoes
1 packet or 4 oz Butter Buds mixed with
¹/₂ c hot water
Salt or salt substitute (optional)
Freshly ground pepper

Bake the potatoes ahead of time, and season and broil the skins just before serving.

Preheat the broiler.

Cut the potatoes in half lengthwise. Scoop out the inside, leaving about ¹/₄ inch. (Save the potatoes to make mashed potatoes for dinner.)

With a sharp knife, cut each potato shell in half, again lengthwise. Brush the flesh side with the Butter Buds. Season lightly with the salt or salt substitute and freshly ground pepper.

Place on a broiling pan, and broil 6 or 7 inches from the heat until brown and crisp—about 5 minutes. Watch closely so that the skins do not burn. Yield: 24 pieces.

Contents per serving (3 pieces):

> *Calories: 48*
> *Sodium: 34 mg*
> *Fat: 0*
> *Percentage of fat to calories: 1 percent*
> *Cholesterol: 0*

You can replace the Butter Buds mixture with nonfat shredded cheddar cheese. Add garlic spice and dip skins into nonfat ranch dressing or nonfat dressing of your choice. You could also top with salsa or dip into the Nacho Cheese Dip recipe. Or you could use nonfat sour cream and add chives to taste.

SPICY POPCORN

2 Tbsp plus 2 tsp reduced calorie margarine
1 Tbsp grated Parmesan cheese
1½ tsp salt-free extra spicy seasoning blend
¼ tsp salt or salt substitute
12 c hot-air-popped popcorn

In a small saucepan, combine the margarine, Parmesan cheese, and seasoning. Blend in salt.

In a large bowl, combine popcorn and margarine mixture. Toss to coat. Yield: 8 servings.

Contents per serving:

> *Calories: 57.7*
> *Sodium: 125 mg*
> *Fat: 2.1 g*
> *Percentage of fat to calories: 34 percent*
> *Cholesterol: .6 mg*

There are many ways to spice up your popcorn. You can try it with garlic powder or onion powder, or instead of Parmesan cheese, try fat-free cheddar cheese.

DIJON CHICKEN SPREAD

> **1 c finely chopped cooked skinless chicken**
> **4 oz nonfat cream cheese, softened**
> **3 Tbsp finely chopped green onion**
> **1 Tbsp Dijon-style mustard**
> **1¹/₂ tsp curry powder**
> **¹/₂ c nonfat or low-fat plain yogurt**
> **1 package melba toast rounds**

In a medium bowl, combine the chopped chicken pieces, cream cheese, onion, mustard, curry powder, and yogurt. Serve with the melba toast rounds. Yield: 14 servings.

Contents per serving:

> *Calories: 19.2*
> *Sodium: 28.3 mg*
> *Fat: .4 g*

Percentage of fat to calories: 18 percent
Cholesterol: 6.2 mg

You could offer an assorted selection of nonfat crackers if you prefer.

This recipe could also be used as a baked potato topper or as a vegetable tray dip. You may consider adding ¼ cup warmed skim milk (just enough to make this recipe creamier, yet not enough to lose the flavor) and placing on 1 cup cooked brown rice or yolkless pasta. Yield: 14 servings.

Remember this recipe for the holidays or special party occasions for an hors d'oeuvre.

SPINACH DIP

2 c nonfat or low-fat plain yogurt
1 10-oz package frozen chopped spinach, thawed and squeezed dry
⅓ c finely chopped fresh onion
2 Tbsp low-fat or nonfat mayonnaise
1 1.4-oz package instant low-sodium vegetable soup mix

In a medium bowl, combine yogurt, spinach, onion, mayonnaise, and vegetable soup mix. Mix well. Serve immediately, or cover and chill up to 3 hours.

You can serve this dip with assorted vegetables, melba rounds, nonfat crackers, or any other low-fat and low-sodium selection of your choice. Yield: 24 servings.

Contents per serving:

Calories: 31.9
Sodium: 448 mg
Fat: .7 g
Percentage of fat to calories: 18 percent
Cholesterol: 1 mg

With many of these snacks and appetizers, you can pack them in small containers and keep them in a cooler when you're on the road.

Chapter 20

A La Carte Dinner and Entree Recipes

These a la carte recipes can be combined creatively to serve yourself or your family and friends an entire meal. Meal combining will allow you to cook lower-fat content meals and still give you a variety for all to enjoy. An a la carte recipe with a snack or appetizer recipe would also be a good combination. Being creative with these recipes will help you and your loved ones stay content without feeling deprived at all. Remember these recipes during the holidays too.

CREAMY PEAS

1 c nonfat or low-fat plain yogurt
2 Tbsp flour
2 Tbsp chopped fresh dill weed or 1 Tbsp
   dried dill weed
2 oz diced pimiento, drained
1/2 tsp salt or salt substitute
1/4 tsp garlic (optional)
1/4 tsp pepper
1 1/2 c fresh or frozen peas
3 Tbsp low-sodium broth

In a small bowl, combine yogurt, flour, dill weed, pimiento, salt or salt substitute, garlic, and pepper. Stir until smooth. Set aside.

In a small saucepan, combine peas and broth. Cover and bring to a boil. Reduce heat and simmer 5 minutes or until the peas are tender. This time will vary depending upon your selection of frozen peas or fresh peas. If possible, use fresh peas.

Stir in the yogurt mixture, and cook over low heat until thickened, stirring constantly. Yield: 4 servings.

Contents per serving:

> *Calories: 99.4*
> *Sodium: 98.4 mg*
> *Fat: .4 g*
> *Percentage of fat to calories: 4 percent*
> *Cholesterol: 1 mg*

With this recipe, you can switch the peas and use diced carrots, broccoli, asparagus, or cauliflower.

CREAMY TURKEY STIR-FRY

12 oz turkey breast tenderloin steak or
   skinless, boneless chicken breasts
1/2 8-oz package nonfat cream cheese, cubed
1/4 c skim milk
1/4 c dry white wine
2 tsp cornstarch
1/4 tsp dried thyme, crushed
1/4 tsp dried chervil, crushed
1/4 tsp salt or salt substitute
1/4 tsp pepper
Nonstick cooking spray
1/2 c sliced celery
1/2 c chopped sweet red pepper
1/2 c chopped onion
1 1/2 c sliced fresh mushrooms
1 tsp vegetable oil
6 oz fettuccine or linguine, cooked and drained

Rinse turkey or chicken and pat dry. Cut into thin bite-size strips. Combine cubed cheese, milk, wine, cornstarch, thyme, chervil, salt, and pepper in a small mixing bowl, and set aside.

Coat a cold wok or large skillet with cooking spray, and preheat it over medium heat. Add celery, chopped pepper, and onion; stir-fry for 1 minute. Add mushrooms, and stir-fry for 1 minute. Remove the vegetables. Add the oil to the wok or skillet. Add the turkey or chicken, and stir-fry for 2 to 3 minutes or until no pink remains.

Add all the vegetables and the cheese mixture. Cook and stir until cheese melts and mixture is heated through. Arrange pasta on a platter. Top with turkey mixture. Serve immediately. Yield: 4 servings.

Contents per serving:

Calories: 187.2
Sodium: 196.3 mg
Fat: 3.5 g
Percentage of fat to calories: 17 percent
Cholesterol: 43.1 mg

TURKEY MEAT LOAF

1½ lb ground raw turkey
½ c sliced green onion
½ c coarsely shredded carrot
¼ c instant potato flakes
⅓ c nonfat plain yogurt
1 Tbsp garlic salt or garlic powder
¾ to 1 tsp poultry seasoning
¼ tsp pepper

2 slightly beaten egg whites
2 Tbsp nonfat mayonnaise or nonfat
  ranch-style salad dressing
2 Tbsp skim milk
1/4 tsp pepper
1/2 Tbsp nutmeg
1/4 c coarsely shredded carrot
2 Tbsp sliced green onion
2 Tbsp sliced onion
2 Tbsp nonfat plain yogurt
Nonstick cooking spray

Combine ground turkey, 1/2 cup green onion, 1/2 cup shredded carrot, potato flakes, 1/3 c yogurt, garlic salt (or, if preferred, garlic powder), poultry seasoning, and 1/4 teaspoon pepper in a large bowl, and stir in the egg whites.

Combine in a very small bowl the mayonnaise or salad dressing, milk, nutmeg, and 1/4 teaspoon pepper. Set aside.

Coat a 9-by-5-by-3-inch loaf dish with the cooking spray. Spoon the turkey mixture into the dish. Use the back of the spoon to smooth the top of the mixture. Bake uncovered in a 350° oven for 1 to 1 1/4 hours or until turkey is no longer pink. In a small saucepan, cook remaining shredded carrot and onions in a small amount of water, covered for 1 1/2 minutes or until vegetables are crisp, yet tender. Drain if necessary. Use 2 spatulas to carefully transfer the meat loaf to a warm platter. Spread remaining 2 tablespoons of yogurt over the top of the meat loaf. Top with carrot-onion mixture. Slice to serve. Yield: 8 servings.

Contents per serving:

Calories: 134.1
Sodium: 102.2 mg

Fat: 5 g
Percentage of fat to calories: 34 percent
Cholesterol: 43.5 mg

TURKEY TACOS

Nonstick cooking spray
1 c chopped onion
1 clove garlic, minced
2 c chopped skinless turkey breast
1 8-oz can low-sodium tomato sauce
1 4-oz can chopped green chili peppers,
  drained
12 taco shells
2 c shredded lettuce
2 medium tomatoes, seeded and chopped
¾ c finely shredded low-fat mild
  mozzarella (or cheddar) cheese

Coat a 10-inch skillet with cooking spray. Add onion and garlic. Cook until tender. Stir in turkey, tomato sauce, and green chili peppers. Cook and stir until heated through.

Divide the turkey mixture among the taco shells. Top with lettuce, tomato, and cheese. Yield: 6 servings (2 tacos per serving).

Contents per serving:

Calories: 314
Sodium: 189.6 mg
Fat: 9.6 g
Percentage of fat to calories: 28 percent
Cholesterol: 79.3 mg

SWISS STEAK

 6 oz lean beef round steak (cut into ³/₄-in
    strips)
 Nonstick cooking spray
 Salt to taste with salt or salt substitute
 1 small sweet potato
 1 medium parsnip
 1 medium onion, cut into wedges
 ¹/₄ c sliced celery
 1 Tbsp quick-cooking tapioca
 1 tsp Worcestershire sauce
 ¹/₂ tsp instant low-sodium beef bouillon
    granules
 ¹/₄ tsp dried thyme or basil, crushed
 ¹/₈ tsp pepper
 1 7¹/₂-oz can tomatoes, cut up

Trim fat from meat, and cut into serving size pieces. Coat a cold skillet with cooking spray. Brown meat in skillet on both sides. Drain. Season the meat lightly with salt or salt substitute.

Peel and quarter the sweet potato. Peel parsnip and cut in half crosswise.

Place the sweet potato, parsnip, onion, and celery in a 1-quart electric slow cooker. Sprinkle with tapioca, Worcestershire sauce, bouillon granules, thyme or basil, and pepper. Arrange meat on top. Pour undrained tomatoes over the meat. Cover and cook on low heat setting for 11 to 12 hours.

Prior to serving, skim off any fat. Spoon sauce over the meat. Yield: 2 servings.

Contents per serving:

Calories: 290.3
Sodium: 547 mg
Fat: 4.6 g
Percentage of fat to calories: 14 percent
Cholesterol: 50 mg

DINNER ROLLS

1½ c all-purpose flour
1½ c whole wheat flour
1 c All-Bran cereal
2 Tbsp sugar
1 package dry yeast
1 tsp dried basil leaves, crushed
1 tsp salt or salt substitute
1 c water
2 Tbsp margarine
2 egg whites
1 c shredded zucchini
½ c shredded carrots
¼ c sliced green onion
2 tsp sesame seeds (optional)
Nonstick cooking spray

Stir together all-purpose flour and whole wheat flour, and set aside. In a large electric mixer bowl, combine the All-Bran cereal, 1 cup flour mixture, sugar, yeast, basil, and salt. Set aside.

Heat water and margarine until very warm (approximately 115° to 120°). Add water mixture and egg whites to cereal mixture. Beat on low speed with electric mixer 30 seconds or until thoroughly combined. Increase speed to high and beat 3 minutes longer, scraping bowl frequently. Mix in vegetables.

By hand, stir in enough remaining flour mixture to make sticky dough. Cover loosely. Let it rise in a warm place until it doubles in volume. Stir down batter. Portion evenly into 12 2½-inch muffin pan cups coated with cooking spray. Sprinkle with sesame seeds if desired. Let rise in a warm place until double in volume.

Bake at 400° about 17 minutes or until golden brown. Serve warm. Yield: 12 rolls.

Contents per roll:

Calories: 156.2
Sodium: 283.8 mg
Fat: 2.3 g
Percentage of fat to calories: 12 percent
Cholesterol: 0

CHICKEN AND BROWN RICE GUMBO

- 1 46-oz can low-salt chicken broth
- 1 lb boneless chicken (roasted), cut into bite-size pieces
- 1 10.5-oz can whole kernel sweet corn, drained
- 1 10.5-oz can stewed tomatoes
- 1 10-oz package frozen okra, thawed and chopped
- ½ c uncooked brown rice
- 1 tsp ground black pepper

In a large saucepan over medium high heat, heat chicken broth, chicken, corn, tomatoes, okra, brown rice, and pepper until mixture comes to a boil. Reduce heat to low, and simmer covered until chicken and brown rice are cooked. Yield: 10 servings.

Contents per serving:

> *Calories: 96.5*
> *Sodium: 174 mg*
> *Fat: 2.1 g*
> *Percentage of fat to calories: 19 percent*
> *Cholesterol: 19.2 mg*

ORIENTAL TURKEY AND BROCCOLI STIR-FRY _____

- 1 c picante sauce
- 1 Tbsp low-sodium soy sauce
- 1 Tbsp water
- 1 Tbsp cornstarch
- ¾ lb boneless, skinless turkey, cut into 2-in strips
- 2 garlic cloves, minced
- 1 Tbsp finely shredded ginger
- 3 tsp peanut or vegetable oil
- 1 tsp oriental sesame oil (optional)
- 1½ c quartered mushrooms
- 1½ c 1-in broccoli florets
- 1 sweet red pepper, cut into 1-in pieces
- 4 green onions with tops, cut into 1-in pieces
- Hot cooked brown rice (optional)

Combine picante sauce, soy sauce, water, and cornstarch in a small bowl. Mix well and set aside.

Toss turkey with garlic and ginger. Heat 2 teaspoons peanut oil and, if desired, sesame oil, in 10-inch skillet over medium high heat. Add remaining 1 teaspoon oil to skillet. Add mushrooms, broccoli, and red pepper. Stir-fry for 3 minutes or until vegetables are crisp, yet tender. Add picante sauce mixture, turkey, and green onions, and cook and stir 1 minute or until the sauce boils and thickens. Serve over brown rice if desired. Yield: 4 servings.

Contents per serving:

> *Calories: 168*
> *Sodium: 479 mg*
> *Fat: 7.5 g*
> *Percentage of fat to calories: 38 percent*
> *Cholesterol: 34.3 mg*

ITALIAN TURKEY KABOBS _____

- 1 lb skinless turkey
- 16 broccoli tips, cooked until crispy, yet tender
- 1 large green pepper, cut into 1-in squares
- 16 mushrooms with the stems removed
- 1 c nonfat, low-sodium Italian dressing
- 8 cherry tomatoes
- 1½ tsp garlic powder (add more or less to your taste)
- 1½ tsp oregano

Slice the turkey into 1-inch chunks, and place into a container. Combine ½ cup Italian dressing of your choice with the garlic and oregano. Take a toothpick and puncture each turkey chunk. Marinate this combination for 1 hour or overnight. (The toothpick puncture allows the flavor of the marinated mixture to soak through the turkey chunks.) While your turkey is marinating, stir the mixture, and toss the chunks as often as possible.

Using 4 kabob skewers, alternately thread the combination of turkey and vegetables. Barbecue the kabobs over coals or on a rack in a roasting pan. Broil or grill for approximately 10 to 12 minutes or until turkey is cooked. Do not undercook or overcook the turkey. While the kabobs are cooking, take 1/2 cup Italian dressing and brush to baste them. Yield: 4 servings.

Contents per serving:

Calories: 172.8
Sodium: 185.7 mg
Fat: 2.7 g
Percentage of fat to calories: 16 percent
Cholesterol: 47.1 mg

This recipe can be altered many ways. Instead of turkey, you may use chicken. The vegetables can also be changed to your favorite selection. You can replace some of the vegetables in this recipe with chunks of peeled and baked potatoes or fresh onions.

STUFFED TURKEY CABBAGE ROLLS

3/4 lb skinless turkey, diced
1/2 c chopped onion
1 c cooked long grain brown rice
1/4 tsp ground cinnamon
1 egg white
6 large cabbage leaves

1 8-oz can stewed tomatoes with no salt
added
1 8-oz can tomato sauce with no salt
added
$1/4$ tsp fresh ground garlic (optional)
$1/4$ tsp pepper

In a medium skillet, brown the turkey and onion until cooked, yet tender. Add rice and cinnamon. Add the combination of seasonings (using any additional saltless seasoning of your choice if desired). Remove from the heat. Stir in the egg white. Precook the cabbage leaves by steaming them or boiling them, whichever is preferred. (The authors suggest steaming them so that the nutrients are not boiled out.) Divide meat mixture among the cabbage leaves, allowing room for the rice to swell. Secure with toothpicks. In a 4-quart saucepan, combine the tomatoes and tomato sauce, and bring mixture to a boil. Reduce heat. Add the cabbage rolls, and simmer uncovered for approximately 30 minutes. Yield: 6 servings.

Contents per serving:

Calories: 124
Sodium: 49 mg
Fat: 1.4 g
Percentage of fat to calories: 10 percent
Cholesterol: 22.8 mg

Turn this into a vegetarian dish by using freshly steamed diced vegetables combined with the other ingredients. Be sure to use brown rice. A vegetarian combination will decrease by a large degree the calorie, sodium, fat, and cholesterol content. But if you prefer, you may use very lean ground beef or ground skinless chicken.

MASHED POTATOES

2 lb peeled potatoes (red or Idaho), cut
   into eighths
4 green onions, sliced
½ tsp curry powder
1¼ c nonfat or low-fat plain yogurt
¼ c low-fat or nonfat milk
½ tsp garlic powder
½ tsp onion powder
2 Tbsp chives
Salt and pepper to taste

Combine yogurt, green onions, and curry powder in a bowl.
Place potatoes in a microwave-safe dish. Add milk. Cover
tightly, and cook on high until the potatoes are tender but
not mushy (approximately 10 to 12 minutes). Remove the
potatoes from the microwave.

Add the yogurt mixture to potatoes, and mash until they are
mixed thoroughly and smoothly. Season with garlic powder,
onion powder, pepper, and salt or salt substitute. Sprinkle
chives over the potatoes in the serving bowl. Yield: 4 servings.

Contents per serving:

Calories: 244
Sodium: 74.5 mg
Fat: .4 g
Percentage of fat to calories: 2 percent
Cholesterol: 1.5 mg

For a cheesy flavor, add more nonfat milk and nonfat cream
cheese.

This recipe can be added to your holiday or special occasion
meal, and you can spice to your guests' taste.

VEGETABLE LASAGNA

- **6 lasagna noodles**
- **2 slightly beaten egg whites**
- **1½ c low-fat or nonfat cottage cheese**
- **⅛ tsp pepper**
- **1 10-oz package frozen chopped broccoli, or 1 9-oz package frozen French-style green beans**
- **4 green onions, sliced**
- **1 c skim milk**
- **4 tsp cornstarch**
- **½ tsp dried dill weed**
- **⅛ tsp pepper**
- **1 c part-skim or low-fat mozzarella cheese**
- **Nonstick cooking spray**
- **½ c grated Parmesan cheese**

Preheat oven to 350°.

Cook lasagna noodles according to package directions. (At specialty stores you can find yolkless lasagna noodles to replace the regular lasagna noodles.) Drain. Rinse with cold water, drain again, and set aside.

Stir together egg whites, cottage cheese, and pepper in a small mixing bowl. Set the mixture aside.

Cook the broccoli or green beans according to the directions on the package, or use the same amount of broccoli or green beans fresh from the produce section and steam until tender. Drain the vegetables and set aside.

For the sauce, in a medium saucepan, cook green onions in ¼ cup water, covered, about 3 minutes or until tender. Do not drain. Combine skim milk, cornstarch, dill weed, and pepper. Add all at once to the green onion mixture.

Cook and stir until bubbly. Cook and stir for 1 minute more. Gradually add mozzarella cheese, stirring until melted. Stir in broccoli or green beans.

Coat a 1½-quart rectangular baking dish with cooking spray. Place 2 of the noodles in the dish. Cut the noodles, if necessary, to fit in the pan. Spread ⅓ of the Parmesan cheese. Repeat layers twice more. Cover the dish with foil.

Bake at 350° for 30 minutes and then remove the foil. Bake for 5 to 10 minutes more or until heated through. Let the dish stand for 10 minutes before serving. Yield: 6 servings.

Contents per serving:

> *Calories: 286*
> *Sodium: 531 mg*
> *Fat: 7 g*
> *Percentage of fat to calories: 31 percent*
> *Cholesterol: 20.6 mg*

Between each layer, you can spread ⅓ can vegetarian nonfat chili for added flavor.

Instead of broccoli or green beans, you can choose another vegetable or add an additional vegetable. Any additional garlic powder or Italian saltless spices can be added to taste.

BROWN RICE STUFFING _____

   2 tsp low-fat margarine
   2 medium tart apples, cored and diced
   ½ c chopped onion
   ½ c chopped celery
   ½ c chopped water chestnuts

½ tsp poultry seasoning
¼ tsp dried thyme leaves, crushed
¼ tsp ground white pepper
3 c cooked brown rice (cooked in 7 cups
   low-sodium turkey or chicken broth)

Melt margarine. Add apples, onion, celery, water chestnuts, poultry seasoning, thyme, and pepper, and stir into margarine. Cook and stir apples and vegetables until they are tender, yet still crisp.

Stir in the cooked brown rice. Cook until thoroughly heated.

Bake in a covered baking dish at 375° for 15 to 20 minutes. Yield: 6 servings.

Contents per serving:

> *Calories: 166*
> *Sodium: 25.5 mg*
> *Fat: 1.5 g*
> *Percentage of fat to calories: 8 percent*
> *Cholesterol: 0*

Instead of baking this recipe, use it to stuff your holiday turkey or roasted chicken. You can find turkeys with no salt or preservatives added instead of turkeys with high sodium content. You may also add mushrooms to this recipe.

SPINACH ENCHILADAS _____

1 small onion, chopped
1 to 2 tsp chopped chili peppers
1 clove garlic, minced
1 Tbsp olive oil

2 c chopped fresh tomatillos, or 2 11-oz
  cans tomatillos, drained and cut up
2 10-oz packages frozen chopped spinach,
  thawed and well drained
¼ c snipped fresh cilantro or parsley
½ tsp salt or salt substitute
¼ tsp pepper
12 6- or 8-inch corn tortillas
2 10-oz cans enchilada sauce
½ c low-fat shredded Monterey Jack cheese
Sliced green onion (to taste)
Nonstick cooking spray

Preheat oven to 350°.

Coat a 3-quart rectangular baking dish with cooking spray. Set aside.

For the filling, in a large skillet, cook onion, chili peppers, and garlic in hot olive oil for 5 minutes. Add the tomatillos and cook, uncovered, over medium low heat for 10 minutes or until the vegetables are tender, stirring occasionally. Stir in the green onion, spinach, cilantro, salt or salt substitute, and pepper. Heat thoroughly.

Wrap tortillas in foil and heat in the oven for 5 to 7 minutes.

Warm the enchilada sauce in a skillet. Dip each tortilla in the warm enchilada sauce about 10 seconds or until limp. Spoon about ¼ cup filling down the center of each tortilla. Roll up.

Arrange the tortillas, seam side down, into the prepared baking dish. Spoon remaining sauce over the top. Sprinkle with the cheese.

Bake in the oven for 15 minutes covered with foil. Uncover and bake for 15 minutes more or until heated through the center. Yield: 12 servings.

Contents per serving:

Calories: 105.5
Sodium: 160.2 mg
Fat: 3.1 g
Percentage of fat to calories: 25 percent
Cholesterol: 2.8 mg

To the filling, you might want to add nonfat mozzarella cheese for a richer cheese flavor.

SALMON CHOWDER _____

- 1 Tbsp low-calorie margarine
- 1/2 c chopped onion
- 1 clove garlic, minced
- 2 c water
- 1 c diced, peeled potatoes
- 1 envelope low-sodium instant chicken bouillon
- 1 8-oz can corn kernels, drained
- 7 oz cooked salmon, flaked
- 1/4 c diced green or sweet red pepper
- 1/4 tsp freshly ground pepper
- 2 c nonfat plain yogurt
- 1/4 c all-purpose flour

In a large saucepan, melt the margarine over medium heat. Add the onion and garlic. Cook and stir 2 to 3 minutes or just until tender. Stir in the water, potatoes, and chicken bouillon. Bring to a boil and simmer, stirring occasionally, 4 to 5 minutes or until potatoes are tender. Reduce heat to low. Add corn, salmon, diced pepper, and ground pepper. Do not boil.

In a medium bowl, combine yogurt and flour, and blend well. Gradually add to soup, stirring constantly, until smooth and slightly thickened. Yield: 4 servings (approximately 5 cups).

Contents per serving:

> *Calories: 279*
> *Sodium: 309 mg*
> *Fat: 5.8 g*
> *Percentage of fat to calories: 19 percent*
> *Cholesterol: 26.5 mg*

Keep in mind with this recipe or any others that have a high sodium content, select the lowest sodium recipes for your breakfast and lunch or in-between snacks for that day. This would be great to put heated in a thermos for lunch or a meal on the road.

VEGETABLE SOUP

> 2¼ c water
> 1 medium potato, cubed
> ¼ c chopped onion
> 3 tsp low-sodium instant chicken bouillon granules
> ¾ c broccoli florets
> ½ c cauliflower florets
> ⅛ tsp ground nutmeg

Combine the water, potato, onion, and bouillon granules in a large saucepan. Bring to a boil and reduce heat. Cover and simmer for approximately 10 minutes.

Stir in the broccoli and cauliflower florets and nutmeg. Simmer about 5 minutes more or until the vegetables are crisp, yet tender. Yield: 2 servings.

Contents per serving:

Calories: 87.3
Sodium: 24.3 mg
Fat: .7 g
Percentage of fat to calories: 7 percent
Cholesterol: 0 mg

This recipe can be altered by using celery, carrots, asparagus, or any other of your favorite vegetables. Any seasoning you like would enhance the flavor.

TURKEY MEATBALLS
WITH SPAGHETTI SAUCE

1 c chopped onion
1 c coarsely chopped green pepper
1/2 c coarsely chopped carrot
1/2 c coarsely chopped celery (1 stalk)
2 16-oz cans salt-free tomatoes, cut up
1 16-oz can salt-free tomato paste
2 tsp dried Italian seasoning, crushed
1/2 tsp sugar
1/2 tsp garlic powder
1/2 tsp salt or salt substitute
2 beaten eggs
2 Tbsp nonfat milk
1/4 c bread crumbs
1/2 tsp dried Italian seasoning
1/8 tsp pepper
1 lb ground low-fat turkey breast (you can
    have the meat department grind
    skinless turkey breasts for the lowest
    fat content)

12 oz pasta, cooked and drained (at a
specialty store, you can find yolkless
pasta)

Sauce

Cook onion, green pepper, carrot, and celery in a covered
4½-quart cooking pot in a small amount of boiling water for
4 minutes or until tender. Drain. Stir in undrained tomatoes,
tomato paste, Italian seasoning, sugar, garlic powder, and
salt or salt substitute. (After this sauce is completed, it will
be important for you to add either salt substitutes or any
additional salt-free spices to flavor to your taste.) Bring to
a boil and reduce heat.

Preheat oven to 350°.

Turkey Meatballs

In a medium bowl, combine 2 beaten egg whites, 2 tablespoons nonfat milk, ¼ cup fine dry bread crumbs, ½ teaspoon dried Italian seasoning, salt or salt substitute, and ⅛
teaspoon pepper. Add 1 pound ground low-fat turkey, and
mix well. Again, you may want to add to this mixture any
additional spices that are salt-free for added flavor.

With wet hands, shape meat into 24 1-inch balls.

Coat a 13-by-9-by-2-inch baking pan with cooking spray.
Place meatballs in prepared pan.

Bake in the oven for 20 minutes or until no pink remains.
Remove, and drain the excess juices.

Add meatballs to sauce. Cover and simmer for 30 minutes.
If necessary, uncover and simmer for 10 to 15 minutes
more or to desired taste and consistency. At this point, add
any additional salt-free seasonings. Some enjoy a mild

sauce, while others enjoy a spicier version. Serve over cooked pasta. Yield: 6 servings.

Contents per serving:

> *Calories: 101*
> *Sodium: 81.3 mg*
> *Fat: .6 g*
> *Percentage of fat to calories: 6 percent*
> *Cholesterol: 47.3 mg*

This recipe can be converted into a vegetarian sauce by replacing the meatballs with vegetables, such as mushrooms or zucchini. You can top your sauce with nonfat Parmesan cheese and serve with a garden salad with the nonfat dressing of your choice.

VEGETABLE PLATE WITH BROWN RICE A LA CHEESE SAUCE _____

- **1 c frozen or fresh brussels sprouts**
- **1 c frozen or fresh carrots, cut up in tiny pieces**
- **¼ c water**
- **2 c cooked brown rice**
- **2 oz shredded nonfat cheddar or Monterey Jack cheese**

Place the vegetables in a steamer or in a saucepan with a metal steamer at the bottom. Steam the vegetables with the water until they are crisp, yet tender.

Drain them and place them on a bed of 1 cup brown rice.

Sprinkle 1 ounce cheese over the vegetables, and let sit for 1 minute or until the cheese has melted. (You can also melt the cheese in your microwave on the lowest temperature setting so that you do not overcook the brown rice. Rice cooked in a microwave can become very sticky.) Yield: 2 servings.

Contents per serving:

Calories: 330
Sodium: 502.3 mg
Fat: 2.4 g
Percentage of fat to calories: 7 percent
Cholesterol: 5 mg

This recipe can be changed in many ways by substituting any of the vegetables or by adding more vegetables. Instead of using the cheese melted on top, you might want to select a nonfat salad dressing or nonfat Parmesan cheese. This recipe can also be spiced differently with a variety of nonsalt selections. You may pack this entree and reheat it at work.

PASTA AND VEGETABLES WITH VINAIGRETTE

1 c sliced zucchini or yellow summer squash
1 small green pepper, cut into bite-size strips
1 clove garlic
1 tsp olive oil or vegetable oil
1^1/$_3$ c corkscrew macaroni or spiral
   spinach macaroni
2 Tbsp white wine vinegar
^{1}/$_2$ tsp dried dill weed
^{1}/$_4$ tsp salt or salt substitute
^{1}/$_8$ tsp pepper
8 cherry tomatoes, halved

Cut the squash in half so there are no large slices. Cook squash, green pepper, and garlic in hot oil in a large skillet about 3 minutes or until tender, yet crisp.

Add the macaroni of your choice (if desired, you may use yolkless macaroni), vinegar, dill weed, salt or salt substitute, and pepper. Toss to mix well. Add tomatoes. Cook and stir until heated through. Yield: 4 servings.

Contents per serving:

Calories: 138
Sodium: 34 mg
Fat: 1 g
Percentage of fat to calories: 7 percent
Cholesterol: 0

This recipe can be altered by adding sweet red peppers or celery. Instead of the vinaigrette, you can use a low-sodium or low-fat Italian dressing. You might want to add chunks of nonfat cheddar cheese or nonfat Monterey Jack cheese to this recipe. Also, you may use several varieties of nonsalt spices to flavor to taste.

SWEET AND SOUR FISH

1 lb frozen fish fillets
$1/2$ tsp low-sodium chicken bouillon
   granules
1 medium green or sweet red pepper, cut
   into 1-in squares
1 medium carrot, thinly bias-sliced
1 clove garlic, minced
2 Tbsp vinegar
4 tsp cornstarch
2 Tbsp low-sodium soy sauce
1 Tbsp brown sugar
$1/2$ c seedless grapes, halved
1 c cooked brown rice

Thaw fish and cut into ³/₄-inch pieces. Place in a 1¹/₂-quart microwave-safe casserole. Microwave, covered, on 100 percent power (or high) for 3 to 5 minutes or until the fish flakes easily. Stir once. Drain and set aside. Be sure not to overcook the fish until it becomes dry and tasteless.

Combine bouillon granules and ¹/₂ cup water in the same casserole. Add green pepper, carrot, and garlic. Cook, covered, on high for 3 to 5 minutes or until vegetables are crisp, yet tender; stir once. Do not drain.

Combine brown sugar, cornstarch, vinegar, and soy sauce. Stir into vegetable mixture. Cook uncovered on high for 1¹/₂ to 2 minutes or until thickened and bubbly, stirring every 30 seconds. Gently stir in fish and grapes. Cook uncovered for 1 minute more or until heated through. Serve over the cooked brown rice. Yield: 4 servings.

Contents per serving:

Calories: 183
Sodium: 78.4 mg
Fat: 1.2 g
Percentage of fat to calories: 6 percent
Cholesterol: 49.9 mg

LEAN SLOPPY JOES

1 lb ground low-fat turkey
¹/₂ c chopped green pepper
¹/₄ c chopped onion
1 8-oz can low-sodium tomato sauce
¹/₂ c barbecue sauce (any bottled variety)

1 c shredded cabbage with carrot
  (coleslaw) mix
8 toasted hamburger buns, or 8 baked
  potatoes

Cook the turkey, green pepper, and onion in a large skillet for 4 to 5 minutes or until turkey is no longer pink. Drain off any excess fat.

Stir in the tomato sauce, barbecue sauce, and cabbage with carrot mix. Bring to a boil and reduce heat. Simmer, uncovered, for 10 minutes.

Spoon some of the turkey mixture onto each bun or potato. Yield: 8 servings.

Contents per serving:

Calories: 216
Sodium: 156.4 mg
Fat: .7 g
Percentage of fat to calories: 3 percent
Cholesterol: 25.5 mg

This recipe can be altered by using skinless ground chicken breast.

To make it vegetarian style, replace turkey or chicken with assorted vegetables that would complement the texture of this recipe. This recipe might require additional salt-free substitute and salt-free spices to taste.

Chapter 21

Desserts

Desserts are rarely included in diets. Since *Gentle Eating* is not a diet book, these recipes are not only good, but they will also allow you to *enjoy* your life-style change. Share these treats with your friends and relatives. They are a good example to people that have given up on diets or people that just have never learned how to cook healthy, lower-fat recipes. In moderation, these recipes are good for holidays and every day.

CHOCOLATE-BANANA CUPCAKES ____

2 c flour
3/4 c sugar
1/4 c cocoa
3/4 tsp baking soda
1/2 tsp baking powder
1/4 tsp salt substitute
1 8-oz container nonfat yogurt
1/2 c mashed ripe banana
1/4 c nonfat milk
1/3 c all-vegetable canola oil
2 tsp vanilla extract
3 egg whites

Heat oven to 350°.

Line muffin pans with foil laminated paper baking cups, approximately 2½ inches in diameter. In a large bowl, stir together the flour, ¼ cup sugar, cocoa, baking soda, baking powder, and salt substitute, and set this mixture aside.

In medium bowl, stir together yogurt, banana, milk, oil, and vanilla. Set aside.

In a small mixing bowl, beat egg whites until soft peaks form. Gradually beat in remaining ½ cup sugar. Beat until stiff peaks form.

Stir yogurt mixture into flour mixture until moistened. Fold ⅓ egg white mixture into flour mixture until moistened, then fold in remaining egg white mixture. Fill muffin cups ¾ full with batter.

Bake 20 to 25 minutes or until wooden pick inserted in the center comes out clean. Yield: 20 cupcakes.

Contents per cupcake:

Calories: 202
Sodium: 58.4 mg
Fat: 2.6 g
Percentage of fat to calories: 55 percent
Cholesterol: .3 mg

STRAWBERRY ICE _____

¾ c sugar
3 c fresh strawberries
¼ c lime juice

Combine sugar and ½ cup water in a medium saucepan, and bring to a boil over high heat, stirring constantly. Remove from heat. Cover and chill thoroughly.

Combine in a blender container or food processor bowl the strawberries and lime juice. Cover and process until mixture is almost smooth.

Stir berry mixture into sugar mixture. Freeze in a 1- to 2-quart ice-cream freezer according to manufacturer's directions. If desired, garnish with lemon and lime slices. Yield: 7 servings.

Contents per serving:

Calories: 98.3
Sodium: 2.5 mg
Fat: .3 g
Percentage of fat to calories: 2 percent
Cholesterol: 0

BANANA-BERRY DELIGHT

1 c nonfat plain yogurt
¹/₂ c orange juice
¹/₂ c fresh or frozen strawberries
1 ripe banana, sliced
2 Tbsp honey
1 Tbsp wheat germ

In blender container, combine all ingredients. Cover and blend on high speed or until smooth. Serve immediately over ice or in frosted mugs. Yield: 2 servings.

Contents per serving:

Calories: 232
Sodium: 90.6 mg
Fat: 1 g
Percentage of fat to calories: 4 percent
Cholesterol: 2 mg

With this recipe, you can substitute the fresh or frozen fruit of your choice.

CARROT CAKE

- ¼ c low-calorie margarine
- ½ c sugar
- 1 egg white
- ¼ c nonfat milk
- ½ tsp vanilla
- ½ c finely shredded carrot
- 1 c all-purpose flour
- 1¼ tsp baking powder
- ¼ tsp ground cinnamon
- ⅛ tsp salt or salt substitute
- 1 dash ground nutmeg
- 2 tsp sifted powdered sugar
- Nonstick cooking spray

Preheat oven to 350°.

Beat margarine and sugar in a mixing bowl until blended. Beat in egg white, milk, and vanilla. Stir in carrot. Combine flour, baking powder, cinnamon, salt, and nutmeg in another bowl. Add to carrot mixture and stir until blended.

Coat an 8-by-8-by-2-inch baking pan with cooking spray. Pour batter evenly into pan. Bake in oven for 20 to 25 minutes or until a toothpick inserted near center of cake comes out clean.

Cool in pan on wire rack for 10 minutes. Remove cake from pan and cool completely.

Place a doily on top of the cake. Lightly sift powdered sugar evenly over the doily. Carefully remove the doily. Yield: 9 servings.

Contents per serving:

> *Calories: 124.9*
> *Sodium: 122.4 mg*
> *Fat: 2.9 g*
> *Percentage of fat to calories: 21 percent*
> *Cholesterol: .1 mg*

BETTER BROWNIES _____

2 Tbsp low-fat margarine
⅓ c sugar
¼ c cold water
½ tsp vanilla
½ c all-purpose flour
2 Tbsp unsweetened cocoa powder
½ tsp baking powder
Nonstick cooking spray
1 tsp powdered sugar

Preheat oven to 350°.

Melt the margarine in a small saucepan, and remove from the heat. Stir in sugar, water, and vanilla. Stir in flour, cocoa powder, and baking powder until well mixed.

Coat the bottom of an 8-by-4-inch loaf pan with cooking spray. Pour batter into pan.

Bake in the oven for approximately 20 minutes or until a toothpick inserted in the center comes out clean.

Cool thoroughly. Remove from pan and cut into bars. Sprinkle with powdered sugar. Yield: 8 servings.

Contents per serving:

Calories: 131
Sodium: 33.1 mg
Fat: 1.5 g
Percentage of fat to calories: 10 percent
Cholesterol: 0

VERY BERRY SUNDAES

4 6-inch flour tortillas
1½ c diced, peeled nectarines
1½ c chopped strawberries
2 Tbsp sugar
½ tsp grated lemon peel
4 scoops or 3 oz vanilla ice milk
1 fresh mint, cut up

Preheat oven to 350°.

Soften tortillas according to package directions. Press each tortilla down into an ungreased 10-ounce custard cup. Bake 10 to 15 minutes or until crisp. Set aside to cool.

Combine nectarines, strawberries, sugar, and lemon peel in a large bowl. Mix gently until well blended.

To assemble, remove tortillas from custard cups. Place each tortilla shell on a dessert plate, and fill with a scoop of ice milk. Spoon equal portion of fruit mixture over tops. Garnish with sprinkles of fresh mint. Yield: 4 servings.

Contents per serving:

Calories: 252
Sodium: 20 mg
Fat: 3.1 g

Percentage of fat to calories: 11 percent
Cholesterol: 2.9 mg

APPLE BAKED CRUMBLE

6 c golden delicious apples, sliced and peeled
2 Tbsp orange or other fruit juice
³/₄ c firmly packed light brown sugar
¹/₂ c all-purpose flour
¹/₂ tsp ground cinnamon
3 Tbsp vegetable oil
Nonstick cooking spray

Preheat oven to 375°.

Coat 2-quart casserole or baking dish with cooking spray. Arrange apples evenly in dish. Drizzle with orange juice.

Combine sugar, flour, and cinnamon in a separate bowl. Mix in oil until crumbly.

Spoon over apples. Bake for 35 minutes or until apples are tender. Cool slightly and serve warm. Yield: 8 servings.

Contents per serving:

Calories: 204
Sodium: 6.5 mg
Fat: 5.5 g
Percentage of fat to calories: 23 percent
Cholesterol: 0

GINGERBREAD COOKIES

Nonstick cooking spray
6 Tbsp unsalted margarine, softened
1 c dark brown sugar, firmly packed

2 large egg whites
$^1\!/_4$ c molasses
$1^1\!/_4$ c all-purpose flour
1 c whole wheat flour
$^1\!/_4$ c dry nonfat milk powder
$^3\!/_4$ tsp baking powder
$^1\!/_2$ tsp baking soda
$^3\!/_4$ tsp powdered ginger
$^1\!/_2$ tsp ground cinnamon
$^1\!/_2$ tsp ground nutmeg
$^1\!/_8$ tsp ground cloves
$^1\!/_2$ c coarsely chopped walnuts (optional)

Preheat oven to 350°. Coat a 12-by-8-inch cookie sheet with cooking spray.

In a large bowl, beat margarine at medium speed until creamy. Add brown sugar, and beat at high speed until light, 1 to 2 minutes. Beat in egg whites. Add molasses, and beat until no lumps remain.

In a separate bowl, sift together flours, milk powder, baking powder, baking soda, ginger, cinnamon, nutmeg, and cloves. Add sifted ingredients to margarine mixture, and blend thoroughly. Stir in nuts, and mix well. The dough will be sticky.

Use 2 tablespoons of dough for each cookie, allowing room to expand. Moisten your fingers before patting the cookie dough flat.

Bake for 18 to 25 minutes. These need to be watched very carefully while cooking. Do not allow the edges to burn. If you desire, moisten cookies. Remove from the oven before they are hardened. Yield: 20 cookies.

Contents per cookie:

> *Calories: 163*
> *Sodium: 29.2 mg*
> *Fat: 5.4 g*
> *Percentage of fat to calories: 29 percent*
> *Cholesterol: .2 mg*

OATMEAL BARS

Nonstick cooking spray
¹/₂ c vegetable oil
¹/₂ c firmly packed brown sugar
1 Tbsp honey
1 tsp vanilla extract
2 c quick cooking oats
¹/₂ tsp baking powder
1 tsp ground cinnamon

Preheat oven to 325°. Coat a 9-inch-square pan with cooking spray.

In a mixing bowl, combine oil, brown sugar, honey, and vanilla. Add oats, baking powder, and cinnamon. Mix until blended.

Press mixture evenly and firmly into prepared pan. Bake 20 to 25 minutes or until edges are golden brown. Cut into 36 squares while still hot. Allow to cool in pan. Store in a container with a loose-fitting lid. Yield: 18 servings (2 squares per serving).

Contents per square:

> *Calories: 121.9*
> *Sodium: 12.6 mg*
> *Fat: 7.1 g*

Percentage of fat to calories: 52 percent
Cholesterol: 0

ALMOND COOKIES

 3 Tbsp unsalted butter, softened
 1/3 c sugar
 3 egg whites
 1 tsp vanilla extract
 Pinch of salt
 3 Tbsp unbleached all-purpose flour
 2 Tbsp cake flour
 1/2 c ground blanched almonds

Preheat oven to 425°. Place the oven rack in the center position. Grease 2 baking sheets well. Sprinkle lightly with water, and shake off the excess. Have handy a metal spatula.

With a hand-held or electric mixer, thoroughly cream the butter and sugar together. Add the egg whites, vanilla, and salt, and continue beating until the mixture is light and fluffy. Add the flours and blend well, then blend in the almonds.

For each cookie, drop 1/2 teaspoon batter onto the baking sheet, spacing well apart, since the cookie will spread. Using the back of a small spoon, spread the batter into 2 1/2-inch circles thin enough to see the ground almonds. Bake, 1 sheet at a time, until the edges are dark brown, about 5 to 6 minutes.

Remove from the oven and let stand for 30 seconds. Then turn the cookies over quickly with a metal spatula. Return the sheet to the oven for 2 minutes more.

Quickly remove each cookie from the sheet, and place almond side up. Place on a rack until completely cooled. Yield: 48 cookies.

Contents per cookie:

> *Calories: 22.7*
> *Sodium: 9.2 mg*
> *Fat: 1.4 g*
> *Percentage of fat to calories: 54 percent*
> *Cholesterol: 2.1 mg*

VANILLA WAFERS

3 Tbsp unsalted butter, softened
¹/₃ c sugar
3 egg whites
1 tsp vanilla extract
Pinch of salt
3 Tbsp unbleached all-purpose flour
2 Tbsp cake flour

Preheat oven to 425°. Place the oven rack in the center position. Grease 2 baking sheets well. Sprinkle lightly with water, and shake off the excess. Have handy a metal spatula and a rolling pin.

With a hand-held or electric mixer, thoroughly cream the butter and sugar together. Add the egg whites, vanilla, and salt, and continue beating until the mixture is light and fluffy. Add the flours and blend well.

For each cookie, drop ¹/₂ teaspoon batter onto the baking sheet, spacing well apart, since the cookie will spread. Using the back of a small spoon, spread the batter into 2¹/₂-inch circles. Bake, 1 sheet at a time, until the edges are dark brown, about 5 to 6 minutes.

Remove from the oven and let stand for 30 seconds. Then turn the cookies over quickly with a metal spatula. Return the sheet to the oven for 2 minutes more.

Quickly remove each cookie from the sheet. Place on a rack until completely cooled. Yield: 48 cookies.

Contents per cookie:

> *Calories: 15.6*
> *Sodium: 9.1 mg*
> *Fat: .8 g*
> *Percentage of fat to calories: 44 percent*
> *Cholesterol: 2.1 mg*

CHOCOLATE PEANUT BUTTER PARFAITS

2 c plus 2 Tbsp cold skim milk
2 Tbsp chunky peanut butter
1 c thawed low-calorie whipped topping
1 package (4-serving size) chocolate flavor
    sugar-free instant pudding and pie filling

Add 2 tablespoons milk to peanut butter, and stir until well blended. Stir in whipped topping.

Pour the remaining 2 cups milk into medium mixing bowl. Add the pudding mix. Beat with a wire whisk until well blended, 1 or 2 minutes.

Spoon the pudding mixture into 6 parfait glasses. Cover with whipped topping mixture. Yield: 6 servings.

Contents per serving:

> *Calories: 147*
> *Sodium: 295 mg*
> *Fat: 6.4 g*
> *Percentage of fat to calories: 39 percent*
> *Cholesterol: 1.4 mg*

CHOCOLATE BALLS _____

1 package moist deluxe devil's food cake mix
2 eggs
¹/₄ c vegetable oil
4 tsp milk
¹/₂ c confectioners' sugar

Preheat oven to 375°. Grease cookie sheets.

Combine the cake mix, eggs, oil, and milk in a large bowl. Stir until thoroughly blended.

Place confectioners' sugar in a small bowl.

Drop rounded teaspoonfuls of dough into confectioners' sugar. Roll to coat and form into balls. Place 2 inches apart on cookie sheet.

Bake at 375° for 8 to 10 minutes or until cooked. Cool 1 minute on the cookie sheet. Remove to cooling rack. Yield: 36 cookies.

Contents per chocolate ball:

Calories: 86.1
Sodium: 124.8 mg
Fat: 3.2 g
Percentage of fat to calories: 69 percent
Cholesterol: 11.8 mg

YOGURT COOKIES _____

1¹/₄ c all-purpose flour
¹/₂ tsp baking soda
¹/₂ tsp grated orange peel
¹/₄ c shortening
¹/₄ c low-calorie margarine

²/₃ c sugar
1 egg
¹/₂ c low-fat vanilla yogurt
1 tsp vanilla extract

Preheat oven to 350°. Grease cookie sheets.

In a medium bowl, combine flour, baking soda, and orange peel, and set aside.

In a large bowl, beat shortening and margarine with electric mixer on medium speed for 30 seconds. Add sugar, and beat on medium speed until fluffy. Beat in egg, yogurt, and vanilla. Stir in flour mixture.

Drop teaspoonfuls of dough, 2 inches apart, onto the prepared cookie sheets. Bake 8 minutes or until golden brown, and remove to wire racks to cool. Yield: 36 cookies.

Contents per cookie:

Calories: 42.9
Sodium: 14.8 mg
Fat: 1.5 g
Percentage of fat to calories: 31 percent
Cholesterol: .1 mg

STRAWBERRY AMARETTI SORBET ____

2 10-oz packages frozen strawberries in
    syrup, thawed
2 tsp fresh lemon juice
1 tsp vanilla extract
3 c fresh strawberries, quartered
2 tsp sugar
2 Tbsp balsamic vinegar
4 Amaretti Italian macaroons, crumbled

Place frozen strawberries, lemon juice, and vanilla in a blender. Blend until smooth about 1 minute. Transfer to ice-cream maker, and process according to manufacturer's instructions.

Transfer the sorbet to a container, and freeze. Place fresh strawberries in a medium bowl. Sprinkle with sugar, and toss. Add vinegar, and toss. Let stand 15 minutes, and stir occasionally.

Scoop sorbet into bowls. Divide strawberries over the sorbet. Spoon over juices left in bowl. Sprinkle crumbled Italian macaroon cookies over strawberries, and serve. Yield: 6 servings.

Contents per serving:

> *Calories: 185*
> *Sodium: 8.8 mg*
> *Fat: 3.6 g*
> *Percentage of fat to calories: 16 percent*
> *Cholesterol: 0*

PEACH CRISPS

Nonstick cooking spray
7 large peaches
2 to 3 Tbsp lemon juice
1 tsp grated lemon zest
Several gratings nutmeg
2 Tbsp unsalted butter
$2/3$ c sifted all-purpose flour
$1/2$ c rolled oats
$2/3$ c tightly packed light brown sugar

Preheat oven to 325°. Coat a 9-by-9-inch ovenproof dish with the cooking spray.

Fill up a small pan with water, and put it on to boil. Dip each peach in the water for 30 seconds, then peel it and remove the pit. Slice the peaches thinly, and put the slices in the prepared dish. Sprinkle with the lemon juice, grated zest, and nutmeg, and toss gently.

Cut the butter into 5 to 6 pieces, and put them in a bowl with the flour, oats, and brown sugar. Mix together, using a pastry blender or 2 knives. When crumbly, spoon the topping over the peaches, trying to cover them evenly.

Bake for 30 minutes or until the peaches are tender. Serve at room temperature. Yield: 6 servings.

Contents per serving:

> *Calories: 242.7*
> *Sodium: 8.3 mg*
> *Fat: 4.7 g*
> *Percentage of fat to calories: 17 percent*
> *Cholesterol: 11 mg*

LEMON RAISIN YOGURT BREAD _____

1¼ c all-purpose flour
¾ c whole wheat flour
4 Tbsp sugar
2 tsp baking powder
½ tsp baking soda
¼ tsp salt
1½ c low-fat lemon yogurt
¼ c unsalted low-calorie margarine,
    melted and cooled slightly
1 egg
¾ c raisins

Preheat oven to 350°. Grease an 8½-by-4½-inch loaf pan.

In a large bowl, combine flours, 3 tablespoons sugar, baking powder, baking soda, and salt.

In a medium bowl, combine yogurt, margarine, egg, and raisins. Stir into dry ingredients until moistened. Pour into prepared pan, and smooth top. Sprinkle surface with remaining sugar.

Bake 40 to 45 minutes or until lightly brown and toothpick, inserted just off center, comes out clean.

Cool in a pan on a wire rack for 30 minutes. Remove from the pan and cool completely, sugared side up. Yield: 12 servings.

Contents per serving:

> *Calories: 153*
> *Sodium: 188 mg*
> *Fat: 3 g*
> *Percentage of fat to calories: 17 percent*
> *Cholesterol: 19.5 mg*

The Gentle
Eating Plan

• gradual changes for permanent weight loss •

1. **Create a safe eating environment
   and a new mental environment.**

   - *gently change how you eat, not what you eat*
   - *the mind-set and the setting often determine how much you eat*
   - *the safer the environment and the better the food, the higher the satisfaction from eating*

2. **Change your schedule to make time for
   exercise.**

   - *night owls can become early birds*
   - *be awake during the time when fewer calories are consumed*
   - *late night television usually means late night calories*

3. **Exercise gently.**

   - *refuse to overdo it*
   - *walking is the easiest way to burn calories*
   - *early exercise starts the metabolism burning calories earlier*

4. **Think like a winner.**

   - *stop the flow of negative thoughts*
   - *attitudes have power to help or to hurt*
   - *brains are reprogrammable computers*

5. **Change the feelings behind the feedings.**

   - *start treating yourself kindly in your head*
   - *unhealed wounds are often medicated with food*
   - *emotional trauma is never overcome quickly*

6. **Replace high-fat foods with foods that are lower in fat.**

   - *finding low-fat, highly satisfying foods is a treasure hunt*
   - *old dogs can learn new habits*
   - *you really can fool yourself about fat*

7. **Lower your intake of foods that are high in sugar.**

   - *fat is the problem, but too much sugar turns to fat*
   - *eliminating sugar eliminates emotional roller coasters*
   - *there is an emotional pattern to eating that can be changed*

8. **Eat more meals a day while taking in the same number of calories.**

   - *the hunger monster gets bigger the longer it goes without food*
   - *hunger monsters can be changed*
   - *fast food usually means fat food*

9. **Work on relationships with things other than food.**

   - *turn hurtful relationships into helpful ones*
   - *feel the gentleness of God*
   - *resolve your past or replicate it*

10. **Find a person or a group to hold you accountable for making healthy decisions.**

   - *you can break the detachment mode*
   - *accountability produces pain you need*
   - *encouragement and confrontation are the keys to accountability*

We want to hear your success stories. Please write to us at:

Stephen Arterburn
P.O. Box 5009
Laguna Beach, CA 92652

Books by
Stephen Arterburn

Addicted to "Love" (Servant)

The Angry Man, Arterburn and David Stoop (Word)

The Complete Life Encyclopedia, Arterburn, Frank Minirth, M.D., and Paul Meier, M.D. (Thomas Nelson)

Drug-Proof Your Kids, Arterburn and Jim Burns (Focus on the Family; rereleased by Gospel Light)

Faith That Hurts, Faith That Heals (originally titled *Toxic Faith*), Arterburn and Jack Felton (Thomas Nelson)

52 Simple Ways to Say "I Love You," Arterburn and Carl Dreizler (Thomas Nelson)

Gentle Eating, Arterburn, Mary Ehemann, and Vivian Lamphear, Ph.D. (Thomas Nelson)

Growing Up Addicted (Ballantine)

Hand-Me-Down Genes and Second-Hand Emotions (hardcover: Thomas Nelson; paperback as *Hand Me Down Genes:* Simon & Schuster)

How Will I Tell My Mother? Arterburn and Jerry Arterburn (Thomas Nelson)

The Life Recovery Bible, Arterburn and David Stoop, executive editors (Tyndale)

The 12 Step Life Recovery Devotional, Arterburn and David Stoop (Tyndale)

When Love Is Not Enough, Arterburn and Jim Burns (hardcover and paperback as *Steering Them Straight:* Focus on the Family)

When Someone You Love Is Someone You Hate, Arterburn and David Stoop (Word)

Winning at Work Without Losing at Love (Thomas Nelson)